PENGUIN BOOKS
METHODS TO GREATNESS

John Aguilar is an award-winning serial entrepreneur, best-selling author, and former decathlon champion. He is the founder and host of the business reality show *The Final Pitch* on CNN Philippines. He sits as president of independent TV production company StreetPark Productions Inc., producer of the long-running real estate and construction show Philippine Realty TV, and CEO of Manila-based venture builder Dragon's Nest. He is the author of the best-selling book *The Art and Science of the Pitch*.

John is a seasoned business and motivational speaker, and has given talks on his experiences as an entrepreneur, TV producer, homebuilder, pitching expert, innovation thinker, and peak performer. He hosts the Methods to Greatness podcast, where he interviews Asia's world-class performers, business leaders, and cultural icons.

John holds an undergraduate degree in Bachelor of Science Psychology from Ateneo de Manila University, a master's in Entrepreneurship from the Ateneo de Manila Graduate School of Business, and is an alum of Singularity University in Silicon Valley. He lives in Manila with his wife and three children.

OTHER BOOKS BY THE AUTHOR

The Art and Science of the Pitch: The Ultimate Playbook for Pitching to Partners, Investors, and Reality TV Shows, Penguin Random House SEA, 2022

Methods to Greatness

Lessons of the Mind, Body, and Soul
from Asia's Top Entrepreneurs, Athletes,
and Icons

John Aguilar

PENGUIN BOOKS
An imprint of Penguin Random House

PENGUIN BOOKS

USA | Canada | UK | Ireland | Australia
New Zealand | India | South Africa | China | Southeast Asia

Penguin Books is part of the Penguin Random House group of companies
whose addresses can be found at global.penguinrandomhouse.com

Published by Penguin Random House SEA Pte Ltd
9, Changi South Street 3, Level 08-01,
Singapore 486361

First published in Penguin Books by Penguin Random House SEA 2022

Copyright © John Aguilar 2022

ISBN 9789814954570

Typeset in Garamond by MAP Systems, Bangalore, India

www.penguin.sg

For Danielle, Luis, and David
May you seek your own paths to find your greatness

Contents

How To Read This Book   ix

Preface   xiii

Introduction   xvii

Act 1: Mind   1

Inbal Arieli   3

Dennis Anthony Uy   14

Dov Moran   28

Jose Magsaysay Jr.   38

Jessica Chen   47

Minh Bui   57

My Mind Journey   73

Act 1: Mind Key Takeaways   75

Act 2: Body   77

Pia Wurtzbach   79

Brandon Vera   90

Toby Claudio   102

Ernest John 'EJ' Obiena   115

Rovilson Fernandez   126

Chien Han How   136

Chot Reyes   143

My Body Journey   155

Act 2: Body Key Takeaways   164

Act 3: Soul   167

Anggun   168

Bryan Thao Worra   175

Gautam Godhwani   186

Bibi Russell   195

Nameeta Dargani   204

My Soul Journey   211

Act 3: Soul Key Takeaways   214

Acknowledgements   217

How To Read This Book

Before we go any further, let's get one thing straight: reading this book will not make you great. In fact, it might even convince you that you're not in such bad shape after all.

Think of this book as a tasting menu. You know you're hungry, but depending on the time of day, what you've eaten last or what you're in the mood for, you will look to this book to fill a particular need or craving. In these pages, you will be presented with portions of wisdom that will give you a taste, but not enough to overwhelm you or fill you up.

Now, imagine you are a chef. The tasting menu will give you an idea of the food and the key ingredients, but it will be up to you to try and make your own interpretation of the dish. It is here to inspire you, and to give you a general idea of how others have done it in the past.

My intention behind interviewing each and every person in this book is to try to learn, pick something up, and apply it in my life—whether it's about business, fitness, routines, or even life goals. The interviewees— from successful entrepreneurs, an Olympian, a TV host, a global recording artist—are wide-ranging and multidimensional. And as much as I've tried to categorize each of them through sections in this book according to how I feel they would add value to the world, they end up surprising me. From the Olympian who has conquered his body, I learned that the mind is the ultimate muscle. From the cerebral inventor of the USB drive, I learned that exercise should be a non-negotiable part of your day. And from a former international model of global brands, I learned the value of slow and sustainable fashion and its impact on communities.

Each chapter begins with an introduction of the person, and then moves to the body of the chapter which is the interviewee talking in first person. In some cases, this takes the form of an interview format.

Fast Talk with John

The chapter then goes to my 'Fast Talk' questions, which I ask all my interviewees on my podcast, the titular *Methods to Greatness*. The questions are as follows:

1. What makes you Asian? What makes you (nationality)?
2. Is there anything from your country (food, place, custom, etc.) that you would like for the world to know about or discover?
3. Who, to you, is a modern-day superhero? What special power does this hero possess?
4. If you could give a commencement speech (if you haven't already), what message would you want to impart?
5. What keeps you up at night? What gets you up in the morning?
6. How do you prepare for what you do? Any special routines you can share?
7. What do you do in your down time? How do you regain focus?
8. What is the one thing you wish you could have known or learned sooner?
9. What would your epitaph say?
10. If there is anything specific you do that you would recommend I try, what would it be?

Questions one and two are an ode to Asia and the interviewee's nationality. It's an invitation for people who are reading this book to explore the vastness of the Asian continent and the richness of our collective culture and heritage.

Questions three and four make the interviewee reflect on a central figure who has inspired them, while imparting a message that will allow them to also inspire others, particularly the younger generation who are in need of Asian role models.

Questions five to seven are an examination of thoughts, hacks, and methods by which our interviewees share how they deal with their own personal struggles and prepare for what they are best at.

Questions eight and nine are perhaps the most pragmatic of the questions and allows us to see the big picture of who the interviewee is and their 'why' or reason for being.

Finally, the last question is the most fun. It is an open invitation or dare, if you wish, for me and you to possibly try something for the first time.

My Thoughts

After the Fast Talk, I give my thoughts as a reaction, whether to validate certain points or give an account of how I have tested certain aspects of what they've shared.

Chapter Assignments

I end with giving you chapter assignments; suggestions on how you can possibly apply some of these methods to greatness. Some are simple and easy, while some are a lifetime commitment. I leave you to imagine how you can build upon your own list.

Disclaimer

I caution you though, that I am in no way a medical or psychology expert and do not intend to dispense any advice that you should do without proper medical supervision. Exercise caution and discretion if you intend to try or do any of the things that you read in this book as it is meant only to guide and not be given as medical or psychological treatment or therapy. My publishers or interviewees or I will not be held liable should you do something that will cause any adverse effects resulting directly or indirectly from any information or advice contained in this book.

On page 90, Miss Universe Pia Wurtzbach gives advice on writing your thoughts down. So, in each chapter, I've also allotted a blank page for notes so you can jot down your crazy ideas that pop into your head from reading the chapter. As Pia says, 'It's never about perfection. It's all about progress, just keeping at it all the time.'

Preface

My first-ever brush with greatness came as a young student-athlete in Manila, Philippines in the mid-nineties. I had just broken the junior record in the 100-metre dash, the most sought-after event in track and field that declared its winner as the 'the fastest man' of the University Athletic Association of the Philippines (UAAP) games.

I broke the record during the preliminaries or heats, taking the advice of my coach, Ed Sediego who told me to just make sure I run a fast but relaxed race so I would have fresh legs for the finals.

Running the 100-metre dash is an oxymoron of sorts. Within the ten or so seconds of running, you are exerting as much effort as you physically can and yet, you are also relaxed and free from strain. You can see this in some of the world's best 100-metre dash performances—the sprinters' faces are stoic but rather than the menacingly intimidating clenched teeth and pained face you expect to see, their facial muscles look completely relaxed—so much so that their facial features seem like loose jello. It is power in its purest form, yet fluid, loose, graceful, and controlled.

I had mentally rehearsed running my races numerous times in my mind, something I had learned to do as a consequence of an unfortunate incident a year prior.

The incident was one of the most important lessons of my life and created such an impact that I take that memory with me to this day.

April 1992. Rizal Memorial Sports Complex, Manila. I was at the starting line of the 100-metre heats in my first track meet. On your mark, get set, then, the bang of the gun—quickly followed by another bang. Someone had jumped the gun, causing a false start.

My fellow competitors and I gingerly moved towards the starting line position. 'On your mark, get set.' And in the split second just before the gun sounded, my mind hesitated; fearing I would be the cause of another false start. The starting gun let out a large bang, and I found myself frozen on the blocks. I looked up and saw my competitors had sped away. The shock was overwhelming, and I ended up hunched and fell flat on my stomach, pounding the track with my hands. I literally looked like a crying baby, and it was not a pretty sight to see.

I had worked so hard in training, only to let myself down by freezing up and not getting off the blocks. As I write this book, I am reminded by my father, who just turned eighty, of that day. 'You froze up and after realizing the others had started without you, you cried in frustration right there at the starting line.' But he also reminded me of the importance of that moment. 'From that point onwards, you learned your lesson, and no one was able to beat you after.'

One year later, I broke the record in the 100-metre dash. I also broke the record in the pole vault and, along with my teammates, the 4 by 100-metre relay record. I later went on to set the junior record in the nationals for track and field's most grueling test: the 10-event decathlon.

That false start propelled me on a path to strengthen not just my body, but my mind. Visualization and meditation would become an integral part of my routine, which helped me learn new skills, take on and be successful at new events. I would do my training in the gym and on the track, but this training would continue and carry over to the school library where I would try to find any resource I could on the sport and on sports psychology.

Looking back, I tried to learn as much as I could as I read up on the stories and routines of my idols: the sprinter Carl Lewis, pole vaulter Sergei Bubka, and decathlete Bruce Jenner, now known as Caitlin. I would imitate their form, their training regimen, and even their approach and mindset towards competing.

I've always said that when I was in school, I learned more things on the track than I ever did in the classroom. We are guided by our parents, our coaches, our peers, and ultimately, we find ways to guide ourselves towards trying to achieve our goals and eventually, our mission. The difference is that when we decide that we want to learn, the world will conspire. As the saying goes, 'When the student is ready, the teacher will appear.'

This thirst for learning continues for me to this day and now the track oval has been replaced by the constantly evolving world of entrepreneurship, and my ever-constant role as a husband and father. As a serial entrepreneur, I am constantly learning and doing research on new industries. As a husband, I continue to strive to grow and evolve with my wife and, as a father, to not just provide but to be a source of strength and inspiration to my children. All this while making sure that I also have time for myself and my own well-being. I've learned that you can never be completely balanced and at certain points, some areas of your life have to and will be compromised depending on what you are working towards achieving at a particular moment in time.

There are many times that I find myself slightly or grossly off-kilter but that, I feel, comes with genuinely trying to stretch ourselves to greatness, and sometimes that can come with a price we have to have the resolve to pay. Even the word greatness itself can be the most subjective of criteria; something that we hoist upon ourselves but never really achieve if not put in its proper context.

These days, I produce and host a business reality TV show called *The Final Pitch* on CNN Philippines, a show inspired by *Shark Tank* and *The Apprentice*. In this show, I am inspired by and learn from so many entrepreneurs—our investor-judges, and startups who pitch on the show. This has been a strong part of my mission through the last couple of years. 'To empower startups and entrepreneurs to be nation builders.'

Deep into the pandemic, I slowly developed the habit of listening to podcasts, in particular, the 'Oprah of Audio' Tim Ferris. He has been successful in building a thriving business and brand that started from his books. *The Four Hour Workweek*, *The Four Hour Body*, *The Four Hour Chef*, *Tools of Titans*, and *Tribe of Mentors* are classic productivity hacks for anyone trying to improve and self-experiment. His podcast *The Tim Ferris Show* has gone on to be much bigger than his books and is now his main revenue driver, if you will, and is often the number one business podcast on all of Apple Podcasts, surpassing 700,000,000 downloads.

Because of Tim Ferris, I decided to produce my own podcast, keeping with the experimental nature that Tim is known for, and something that resonates with my adventurous spirit. Later on, I stumbled upon another podcast, Lewis Howes' *School of Greatness*, a podcast that has helped tremendously in improving my life and been instrumental in inspiring my own passion projects, such as the podcast and this book.

I am also learning from my interviews on my podcast, *Methods to Greatness* from which this book gets its title from. *Methods to Greatness* is a product of the pandemic. This book is actually a product of a pitch I made to the publisher for the upcoming *Methods to Greatness* podcast, on which the book was to be based upon. So technically, the book deal was signed even before I came out with the podcast that would be the basis for this book. So, in a way, I guess you can say I had created the chicken and the egg at the same time and found a way to make them both happen.

I did not make any serious attempt to reinvent the wheel. What worked for Tim is that he has gone on to not just interview but actually test and try out for himself the advice he was given. The human guinea pig that is Tim sits well with how I actually also try things out for myself. I really will try anything at least once and in this book, I make similar attempts that are works in progress. The book and podcast were a perfect excuse to try things out for the first time, and to also be accountable to not just myself but to people I share these forays into the unexplored with.

The biggest difference between the works of Tim Ferris, Lewis Howes, and me is that I write this book from the Asian perspective. In choosing my interviewees, they are either Asians, residing in the Asian continent, or are of Asian descent.

Another big difference is that I also write this book from the perspective of being a husband and father. Asians in general, even across the diaspora, are known to keep very tight familial bonds. There are many insights in this book that I share of how family plays an integral role in our overall well-being and happiness.

In this book is an eclectic mix of characters, people whom I have sought out because I admire, respect, and value their contributions to society and to the world. They are by no means perfect, but it is in their imperfection and willingness to grow and thrive amid their limitations that make them truly great.

Introduction

'There is no such thing as work-life balance—it is all life. The balance has to be within you.'

—Sadhguru

The book is divided into three sections: Mind, Body, and Soul. In each section, I share with you interviews I've had with people who have achieved mastery in these aspects of the human condition.

You will find that though I've divided my subjects and 'categorized' them perhaps because of what they are primarily known for or what their profession dictates they should be good at, a lot of them deal with subjects that cross over, even attributing their success to something that is beyond their perceived sphere of expertise.

Filipino Olympian pole vaulter EJ Obiena, for instance, has been an athlete all his life, but through all his years of training has attributed a drastic improvement not from a physical, but a mental adjustment that has allowed him to be the best Asian pole vaulter in history, and one of the best in the world.

Bibi Russell, a top Bangladeshi fashion icon and one of the most prolific supermodels of her generation, was known for her beauty and physical attributes, but has transitioned to giving opportunities for communities to benefit from her business, and her humanitarian efforts have truly shown not just her physical endowments but her compassion and generosity of her soul.

And Israeli Dov Moran, the brilliant mind behind the invention of the USB drive, now a prominent and prolific investor, harps on the absolute necessity of staying physically active and constantly moving. He never takes a call sitting down, walking anywhere between 15,000–25,000 steps a day. He is completely vegetarian.

The sections are not mutually exclusive and you will find in these interviews the constant striving for the balance of the mind, body, and soul.

We each have our own demons, and our own dreams and aspirations. In these pages you will find Asians who have been inspired to achieve their own greatness as seen by people like me who admire them. They are world class athletes, successful entrepreneurs and tycoons, and cultural icons. As you will see, they are also real people like you and I who grapple with their own demons and everyday challenges.

Though most of the people I've interviewed for this book lead extraordinary lives, there's something for everyone to learn from how they've achieved greatness. Whether you're an entrepreneur or an employee, mother, student, or a student of life. There's bound to be something here that will nurture your mind, body, and soul. Allow me to share this journey of discovery and self-discovery with you.

Namaste!

Act 1: Mind

'If your mind is empty, it is always ready for anything; it is open to everything. In the beginner's mind there are many possibilities; but in the expert's mind there are few.'

—Shunryu Suzuki

Whenever I enter a room full of people, I am always excited with what I can learn collectively from each person. Instead of speaking, I would much rather listen. The best and most fascinating rooms are the ones I enter where I realize that I am absolutely the dumbest person there. Ego aside, there is nothing more liberating than intellectual humility, as it allows my mind to be open to a spectrum of ideas.

In this section, I've curated and put together a room full of people with whom I have deep respect for how their minds work.

Inbal Arieli is a founder of a global leadership assessment firm and book author. She defined for me the Israeli trait '*chutzpah*' and how it has helped Israel become the startup nation.

Chinese immigrant Dennis Anthony Uy migrated from poverty from China to the Philippines and rose to become one of the country's fastest rising tycoons. I learned that his overnight success was decades in the making.

Kenichi 'Kent' Yoshida gave me a sneak peek into the boardroom of Softbank and how to balance the legendary investor Masayoshi Son's penchant for 'crazy' ideas, and Kent's counterbalance of practicality.

Dov Moran, the inventor of the USB flash drive, shares his earliest memories of how his invention has changed the lives of people from around the world.

1

Emmy Award-winning former journalist Jessica Chen teaches me how to balance traits East and West to be a better communicator.

And finally, I sharpen my entrepreneurial mindset by learning from the different businesses of entrepreneurs from different industries: food franchise king Jose 'Jomag' Magsaysay, multi-industry millennial serial entrepreneur Minh Bui, and medical entrepreneur James Soh.

There are common themes such as innovation, focus, and the value of failure in business. Yet there are other gems such as letting our children play unsupervised, not asking questions but having a conversation instead during an interview, and the value of psychotherapy, that are springboards for deeper reflection.

I hope that as you enter the room, you enjoy each conversation and learn from these brilliant minds too.

Inbal Arieli

Founder, Synthesis, a global leadership assessment firm
Author, *Chutzpah: Why Israel Is a Hub of Innovation and
Entrepreneurship*

**'I know what works for me today, it is not what worked
for me back then and what will work for me ten years from now. It is
all about our flexibility and willingness as human beings
and individuals to evolve.'**

Don't be afraid to make mistakes

*Born in Israel and raised on hummus and chutzpah, Inbal fostered her entrepreneurial
skills during her mandatory military service, serving as a lieutenant in Unit 8200, the
Israel Defence Forces' elite intelligence corps.*

After completing her military duties, and for the past twenty plus years, Inbal embraced leading executive roles in the flourishing Israeli tech sector and has founded a series of programmes for innovators, where she currently holds board seats.

Inbal is also widely known as the author of Chutzpah: Why Israel Is a Hub of Innovation and Entrepreneurship, *the book that gave the world a sneak peek into why Israel, a tiny country that's barely the size of New Jersey, has produced so many successful startups, earning it the title of Startup Nation. The book has already been translated into various languages.*

Inbal lectures widely to business and government leaders around the world, analysing and discussing the most critical leadership skills, based on how Israeli culture breeds risk-taking and entrepreneurship from the very young age of four. Among her most popular keynotes are 'Chutzpah: Skills for the Future', 'From Special Forces to the Board Room', and 'The Secrets of Successful Interviewers'.

Inbal holds an LLB Law, BA in Economics and an MBA, all from Tel Aviv University. She was also featured as one of the one hundred most influential people in Israeli tech and as one of the top one hundred tech business women speakers in the world.

On Methods to Greatness, Inbal graciously shared with us insights from her book, lessons she learned during her time in the military, and how the Israel Defence Forces is helping the Israeli startup scene, the importance of nurturing risk-taking, creativity, resourcefulness, and teamwork in young kids, and ways on carving success out of chaos through the Israeli 'balagan' concept.

On her book *Chutzpah: Why Israel is a Hub for Innovation and Entrepreneurship*, and how kids can build an innovative mindset

When I was writing the book, I had a dilemma: what is it more of, a parenting book or a business book? My playground is the business space and it is a business book, but the anecdotes, analogies, and the stories that I bring in the book are actually inspired by childhood.

The involvement, development, that happens throughout our childhood that trains our soft-skill muscles are truly trained from a very young age. In the typical Israeli playground, you just let kids play in a free environment without too much guidance. That's the point there. You do not guide them or instruct them too much on how to play, on how to act. We're used, as adults, to having best practices to follow, to relying on past experience, but with kids, if you don't share with them the best practices, they will either find best practices of their own or they would be the one to realize what these are. And so, in Israel, in a typical playground where you have the average slide, you will see Israeli kids at the young age of two to four just doing whatever they want.

I spent my childhood in Switzerland; I was taught, instructed, guided by adults to climb up the ladder and sit on my bottom and come down the slide. In an Israeli typical playground, you would also see kids doing that, but there are also kids climbing up the slide. You would also see kids just standing in the middle of the slide and waiting for other kids to go under their legs like a bridge, you would see kids jumping from the slide—and why not? They're all having fun playing and it's an enjoyable moment for them and they are just doing it in a different way than us adults would want them to.

We look for control, for predictability, for certainty, for order, which creates more comfort and confidence for us. But it is not how kids are actually wired at that age; and so an external observer of an Israeli playground would see kids running all over—a lot of noise, jumping, bumping into each other, yes, but they figure it out by themselves. They confront these small conflicts, they learn how to resolve them, and there's an entirely different rhythm, and tempo to an Israeli playground. To me, this is an example of creativity and risk-taking management and teamwork, and coping with uncertainty, and that's where it starts—on this simple slide in a playground.

On preparing kids for the unknown

I am a parent of three boys. They don't play in a playground any more but they used to, and that parenting instinct of wanting to protect your kids is, of course, natural. The question is: what is our role as parents? Is it to do everything for our kids and protect them, or is it to train them and equip them with the ability to cope with what the world has in store for them?

I think the COVID-19 pandemic showed us that we don't control everything, anywhere, any time; we just convince ourselves that we do, but we don't, really. So, I think it is all about, of course, wanting to protect your kids and wanting them to have the best life they can have, but understanding that your role as parents is to enable that—to find their own way to train and equip them with the right mindset. That's why I use the term 'muscles' so much because I think the mind is trainable. I think it is something that we can practice over time and become more familiar with. With our ever-changing world, we don't really know what the future of our kids would look like, in the Philippines, in Japan, in Vietnam, in the US—we don't really know what it would look like 10–15 years from now. Preparing for the unknown is a tough mission, but it is all about fostering and practicing these skills within the kids.

On the influence of the Israeli Defence Forces (IDF) on the country's startup scene

The IDF is a very unique military organization and, in a way, it is different from what people have in mind when they imagine the military organization. It is built in a different way, it is managed in a different way, it operates in a different way. The result of that is when former soldiers leave the military after three or four years of service, they become very entrepreneurial and innovative, and they are accustomed to using or designing technology.

So, surprisingly, in a sense, the military is a hotbed of innovation. However, we join the military at the age of eighteen, and we bring into the military a toolbox, a set of mindsets and principles—muscles, if you want—or soft skills that we have developed throughout our childhood. I think the combination of that unique childhood journey and then the setting that the military provides actually creates so much innovation, so much entrepreneurship, resulting in soldiers joining the tech industry after their military service.

Here are military principles that can and, in my opinion, should be applied to the business world: the screening process starts at around the age of sixteen and a half, and throughout that last year of high school, you go through a variety of interviews, tests, and screening stages—not much, by the way, because you're in high school and you're actually going through your exams. The military gets access to your very limited time, so the screening process would be effective in terms of the time investment that they require from you.

With the fact that you're only sixteen and a half or seventeen, you don't really understand what you're about to experience in the military and what that means. At the age of seventeen, there is just nothing relevant in your CV to a military organization. That lack of background of experience, or knowledge, has actually turned into an advantage in the screening process because that actually means that you are not focusing on what you already know, but on your potential and what you could learn and what you could turn into.

On how to create a company culture where failure is seen as productive

Today, we celebrate a lot of successes and are more concerned about mistakes and failures. We prefer to celebrate the successes and the positiveness of everything. However, if we are incapable of looking failure right in the eye and realizing our mistakes, we can't learn from them. So, I think that it is about finding your inner motivation. When I speak to young entrepreneurs, I tell them to always be open to external feedback and hear others. It is critical to always remember what is important to them, why they are doing what they're doing, and why they made those decisions—and to reconnect back to their inner self and inner motivations. It is not an easy task, but it is a very important one and once you are able to do that, I think you are able to be more open, to understand mistakes and failures.

So, the idea is, how do you create a culture that not only encourages people to think for themselves, to not be afraid of making decisions, to learn from mistakes? If we want them to rely on themselves by making decisions, we need to provide them a setting where they can make mistakes; otherwise, they would be too afraid to decide. If we're willing to provide them a setting where they can make mistakes and learn from their mistakes, it would be an open and trusted environment where one can admit mistakes and learn from them. We need to work in teams because we cannot rely on one person alone. And, going back to the military, what would ever motivate a nineteen-year-old kid to make decisions and be responsible with the big things? It is actually the fact that they are heard, that their opinions matter.

If you think about the growth of a company, yes, you can think of some senior executive guiding the way or even telling you what to do, but the more you bring voices from the bottom, lead their voices, and connect it to action and accountability, then you can actually make a connection between motivation and drive, and creativity and trust and teamwork—and suddenly all these components come together for a more holistic organization. The Israeli military does that out of necessity, because of the way it relies on 18–19-year-old kids; they will not be motivated just because they were told what to do.

On having a strong sense of community while having a global mindset

Israel is a tiny country; it is a very small market. That's why Israeli startups are addressing the global market scene, because the market here is just too small for them. You need to find some bridges for the different markets and there are different ways of doing that. There is a very strong community in Israel; in my book, I show, in Hebrew, that we are actually from the same root. You will always become part of something greater than yourself. Your sense of belongingness, to this greater thing, the state, the people is always present. We have seen a growing network of Israelis in different places around the world, and we have different Israelis living there for good or for a shorter period of time, and they are always there connecting bridges for the ones that are still here in Israel. You immediately have a lending hand willing to help you. In the tech ecosystem, it is important because this is how you get introduced to investors, this is how you meet new talent who may want to hire your company to your clients, and it works pretty well.

On the Israeli way of pitching business

I think if there's one thing that we could learn is the Israelis' agile or flexible way of pitching. When you work with a US-based startup accelerator, there would be very clear best practices and guidelines and structures that actually work on creating the right pitch. Startups would actually go to this checklist, and they would typically learn it by heart. They would know it, press play in the middle of the night, and they would know what to say at any given moment. And it works. What does not work there, is when you need to adapt that pitch to the nuances of the person you are pitching to. I think that is what works for Israelis in their chaotic balagan pitches.[1] They don't put too much emphasis on the structure or having that clear narrative or one-size-fits-all pitch; what they do is they come into a conversation. And so, their pitch would sound differently to a client versus an investor versus a tech-savvy client, and they would do it not because of strategy; they would do it because they are coming into a conversation. And that can be much more adapted to the person, the human being in front of them—and that actually is the important element in pitching.

On how grit leads to success

There is no formula. I don't have one solution; I think it really depends on where you have a set of elements, they are all present in the equation or the formula and they have different weights. And in that different combination of different weights of different elements. The result would be different for each person. So my answer is that I know what works for me today, it is not what works for me back then and what will work for me ten years from now. It is all about this flexibility and willingness as human beings and individuals

---

[1] *Balagan* is a Hebrew word that means chaos or disorder.

to evolve, so I think the most important part of grit is the willingness and openness just to develop and evolve that we are not the same person throughout our lives.

On how to conduct an effective interview

1. **Don't just ask questions—have a conversation.** When most people think of an interview, they think: you have a set of questions, you answer that set of questions, and you're mostly focused on getting answers to all these questions. My first tip is that any interview should not be a set of questions; it should be a conversation. Do your prep work, be ready, think of the questions you want to ask and have that list with you, but don't feel that you need to check all those questions. Because by doing that, the flow is going to be completely ruined, and you may miss so many interesting things.

2. **Don't talk too much.** People often become too busy talking, and that's counterintuitive. For example, in hiring interviews, if you are the interviewer, the more you speak, the better you will think the candidate is, because when you hear yourself speaking, you hear what you want to hear. So, practice doing as little talking as possible and use most of the time for other purposes.

3. **Accept the pauses.** What do we do with silence? When you pause for a second and there's silence, the interviewee would be able to think more deeply and formulate more insights.

4. **Shake up the dynamics.** Let's say, for example, a Venture Capital (VC) Fund interviewing a team for due diligence would say, 'Okay what questions do you have for us?' Many entrepreneurs have tactical questions about the process, but very few entrepreneurs would ask the important and relevant questions: 'Why would you want to invest in us?', 'What do you think we could do better?' By shaking up the dynamics, you also get how they think.

5. **Examine your emotions.** We are often focused on the data we collect. What she answered, what she said, what she chose not to answer. But what feelings did you invoke in the interview? Most feelings that were invoked say something about the conversation; if you interviewed someone and they made you tense or stressed, there's a reason, it is not by coincidence. It is important to focus not just on the data itself; it is also important to understand the experience of the conversation.

Fast Talk with John

What makes you Israeli?

Everything in my life: the food I eat, the trees in our backyard, the language in which I dream at night, the music I listen to and the books I read, my optimism, energy, and wish for a better world for all. The small moments in my day-to-day life, combined with a greater mission—all of these make me Israeli.

Is there anything from your country (food, place, custom) that you would like the world to know about or discover?

The Mediterranean beaches of Tel Aviv, packed with diverse people pumped with energy and positive spirit. There's no place like Tel Aviv!

Who, to you, is a modern-day superhero? What special power does this hero possess?

The balancing power. My superhero is capable of combining different elements in life, in a variety of topics and practices. A little bit of this and a little bit of that. Whatever 'this' and 'that' are.

If you could give a commencement speech (if you haven't already), what message would you want to impart?

Stay positive, act proactively. Be humble and kind. And make sure to ask—others, but mostly yourself—a lot of questions. All the time.

What keeps you up at night? What gets you up in the morning?

I enjoy sleeping as well as dreaming. Sleeping has always been important for me.
    And it's our two dogs that wake me up early every morning for their morning walk.

How do you prepare for what you do? Any special routines you can share?

It depends on the activity or task. However, what's common to all is that I try to be present in the moment, totally focused. My mobile will often be on do not disturb (DND) mode so there are no distractions.

What do you do in your downtime? How do you regain focus?

I take a break, drink an espresso, mobile on the side. For approximately five minutes, I do nothing.

What is the one thing you wish you could have known or learned sooner?

That most of the decisions in my career are not as fateful as they seem.

What would your epitaph say?

Loved the world. Loved the people in her life. Loved every moment of her life. Loved.

If there is anything specific you do that you would recommend that I try, what would it be?

Headstand. For over five minutes. On a daily basis. Enjoy!

My Thoughts

I was first introduced to who Inbal is when the Israel Embassy in the Philippines sent me a copy of her book, *Chutzpah*. Along with another book *Start-Up Nation*, the two books represented perhaps the story that Israel wanted to portray. To be one of two books that your embassy will recommend for people to read about your country is quite an honour.

I interviewed Inbal for my podcast and for this book on Zoom, and one of the things that stood out from that conversation was her warning that we may hear sirens in the background at any point and that we should not be alarmed as it was apparently quite a normal occurrence.

On a recent trip to Tel Aviv, I finally got to meet Inbal in person. She, along with her programme manager at Chutzpah Centre, Daniel, took me to a nice little French restaurant near her office along Rothschild Boulevard. My first book under my publisher Penguin Random House SEA, *The Art and Science of the Pitch*, was just about to be released and I wanted to pick her brain and seek advice on how she has successfully navigated the challenges and opportunities of being an internationally published author.

The first thing she asks upon seeing me is if I heard the sirens that sounded off a couple of hours ago. 'We were worried for you that you might panic given what I've told you,' she said. I assured her that I didn't even notice the sirens as I was engaged in a meeting at that time.

To begin with, Inbal, like me, is not in the business of being an author. We are both serial entrepreneurs and our books are an extension of ourselves, of the worlds we navigate given our businesses and fields of experience and expertise. We give talks and keynotes, but only if it makes sense to our objectives and impact they can create.

One thing I learned from Inbal during that lunch that stuck, is her ability to position herself as a thought leader. She talks to me about one of her projects, The Founders Studio, a series of twelve identical questions she introduces to the most interesting people she meets in different communities. There is a series on 'Israel's Tech Role Models', and another on 'Extraordinary Women in Tech'. The questions are short, to the point, and the whole thing probably won't take you fifteen minutes to answer. When I asked her the reason why she came up with the project? 'It's fun!' I then venture the possibility of it also being a book, to which she says it can be that at some point. Make no mistake about it though, The Founders Studio is an excellent curation of minds and thought leadership at its best.

Inbal likewise shares about her experience promoting her book, *Chutzpah*. On a US book tour for her New York-based publisher Harper Business, she went, alone, to twelve states in fifteen days. As we were well into our chicken schnitzel main course, her programme manager Daniel informs her of a high-profile foreign delegation that is asking for a keynote to be scheduled during their visit to Tel Aviv. Inbal has created a very powerful voice and identity with her book, and I can imagine the ride to be both exhilarating and rewarding.

Upon arriving back to Manila from my trip, Daniel sends me an email inviting me to take part as a Chutzpah Ambassador, a non-obligatory role they have extended to people from around the world, essentially involving them in the spread of the Chutzpah mindset. 'I graciously accept,' I replied to Daniel. 'Let's start things off with my upcoming book *Methods to Greatness*.'

Chapter Assignments

It's natural for us to want to regain control of our lives when we've been so busy with the day to day and the responsibilities of it all. However, as Inbal recommends, try to see the beauty in chaos—and see how you can work that to your advantage.

- Take a leap of faith on something you've always wanted to do. Make sure it's something that will contribute to your own personal development. Go skydiving, pick up an unusual hobby, or ask that girl or guy out. And don't take the task—or yourself—too seriously.
- Teach the kids in your family to have a more innovative mindset. Allow them to play more freely and let them loose without giving any instructions or limitations on what they can or cannot do. Empower them to resolve issues on their own rather than hovering over them and feeding them the answers.
- In your company, instead of a 'Suggestion Box', why don't you try something new like a 'Most Spectacular Failure' of the month or week. And instead of being reprimanded, celebrate this failure. You can make it a regular affair that incentivizes creative thinking and moving outside your boundaries.

Dennis Anthony Uy

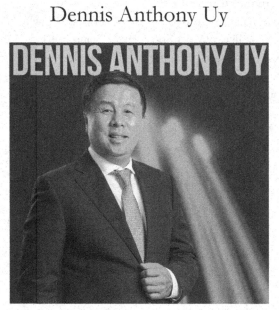

Cofounder and CEO of Converge ICT Solutions, Inc.

**'It's not just about profit; the profit will come
when you do something good.'**

Running a business is about serving your country

*Dennis Anthony Uy is the cofounder and CEO of Converge ICT Solutions, one of the
Philippines' leading internet providers, after pursuing the broadband and fiber optics
industry way back in 1996. Almost three decades since, Dennis and his wife and Converge
cofounder Maria Grace surprised the Philippines' business scene when they debuted in the
Forbes Asia's top fifty richest Filipinos list, ranking at a high number six in 2021.*

Despite being a foreigner who had to grow up in a country completely different from his homeland China, Dennis' vision as an entrepreneur has always been deeply rooted in serving the Filipino people by making connectivity affordable and accessible for everyone.

Dennis migrated to the province of Pampanga in 1970 when he was just eleven years old, following his parents who made the move a year before he did because of the cultural revolution happening then in China.

Through the help of an uncle, Dennis, along with his siblings, was able to finish his public-school education, which he did so while working at his uncle's grocery store as an all-around employee overseeing the cashier, sanitation, and security.

From having zero knowledge of the local language, Dennis also became fluent in the local dialect Kapampangan and, eventually, Tagalog, as he grew up in Angeles City.

It was in his youth when Dennis cultivated his passion for electronics, starting with programming games such as PacMan and other Atari titles, as well as betamax and VHS tape machines, and fixing these machines for his uncle's store. He pursued his passion further by taking up an electronics course, and his first entrepreneurial venture was to duplicate movies on VHS and betamax and rent them out in his community.

When these tapes started to go out of fashion, Dennis changed his business strategy and established his own cable TV company, setting up the necessary antenna connections himself for his customers in Pampanga. A pivotal moment for Dennis was when the 1990 Mount Pinatubo eruption happened—with his community struck by this unexpected disaster, and despite everyone leaving because of the devastation brought about by the lahar and extreme ashfall, he decided to stay and to continue providing his hometown with news and entertainment while strengthening his communication infrastructure in the area.

From cable TV, Dennis saw an opportunity in the fiber optic network industry in 1996 as Clark, Pampanga, started to emerge as an economic zone. Anticipating the businesses this area would attract, Dennis started acquiring smaller cable companies to widen his company's coverage, all while selling electronic hardware to schools and offices.

Fast forward to today, Converge now prides itself as the first end-to-end fiber internet network in the country. Now that the new normal continues to encourage people to do most activities at home, demand for bandwidth is greater than ever—and Dennis Anthony Uy is here to ensure that Converge is ready to provide Filipinos with efficient connectivity, wherever they are in the country.

On building a company with one's spouse

Grace and I got married in 1997. We met each other through common friends; she worked in IBM before, and she's a CPA. And when you're a CPA, you work with multinationals and you are used to a system, a structure. With me, everything is the opposite, totally. I don't have control, I'm just the tech guy who's passionate about technology, I want to roll out this and go in massively and without control. So, our relationship is the perfect combination, right?

After we got married, she decided to join us in the company to help me. When we started, she took care of the business to put a system in place. We have 4,000 people now.

On venturing into a competitive market

When you enter Metro Manila, It's not easy. You get boxed out by the big giants; it's challenging. So, when I targeted Metro Manila, I did it through a partnership with others—first with Destiny Cable.[2] I contributed consumer technology, then I saw the opportunity in the enterprise segment, which they didn't have. I introduced my expertise and it became value-added revenue for them by using the existing infrastructure to deliver to this enterprise market.

In the middle of this transaction, Skycable acquired them.[3] So this got me in a bit of a panic and I needed to think about how quickly I could roll out my own infrastructure. At that time, I had just gotten the franchise from Congress. Finally, we got our licence in, in 2009 and 2012. I needed to think of a way to circumvent any challenges, so I went to a lot of technology shows outside the country. For a number of years, I was the only Filipino attending these high-tech shows of society cable engineers in America, the Fiber Home Council. From these you can learn a lot about best practices in the industry because you meet a lot of people.

On choosing your investors

During the Converge media launch in 2016, what I envisioned for Converge and what's happening today in the industry is 100 per cent the same. So that's six years ago, almost. I said that we would only have 100,000 fiber subscribers by then, PLDT, maybe 200—that's only 300,000 fiber subscribers.[4] So, I said, with the size of the Philippines, we would need this kind of digital infrastructure. The market, the technology, everything was there, and I had a track record for a number of years already. The only piece lacking for me was

---

[2] Destiny Cable was the second-largest cable TV provider in the Philippines. It was eventually acquired by Skycable.

[3] Skycable (or Skycable Corp.) is a major Filipino telecommunications company.

[4] PLDT, Inc. is one of the Philippines' major telecommunications providers.

the money to push this. In 2018, I had another launch and I invited all the big foreign telecoms, and even banks, to find my investors. Then, I talked to SubCom US to be able to build submarine cables. Imagine, as early as 2018, submarine cables were in my plans. Today, everything is finished. So, you need three to four years to design, plan, and then execute.

I announced that to the public without money but we already had some revenue already. My revenue then was just only I think close to ₱2 billion, which is totally incomparable to what we have today, which is 10–15 times more—in just a span of three years. I pitched to the venture capitals, sort of like a beauty contest, where I laid out all my credentials, my technology, my successes, my roadmap and projection and everything. I presented to these investors, all of them were willing to put out. But I didn't need just the money; more than that, I needed to see how they could contribute to my company, if they have a track record in the same industry. Finally, we selected Warburg Pincus. That seal of approval is also very important; for a private equity firm like Warburg Pincus, being 100 years in the business, to put money in your business, that's a seal of approval, because of all the due diligence and scrutiny that you will have to go through and pass.

On his vision for Converge's development in the Philippines

I want to see how we can use technology to uplift the Filipino. That's very important because nowadays, you can see all over the world, all these successful countries have a combination of technology and talented people who are able to uplift their lives faster. Even during my early days, it was not just about profit; the profit will come when you do something good. People will appreciate and help you and once they see you are successful, I tell you, private equity, venture capitals, when they see your product and you as a passionate entrepreneur, the money will follow.

Down the road, I need to develop different adjacent, supporting businesses. We have that digital highway with our fiber optic connections to individual homes; in due time, we will be reaching 3,000,000–4,000,000 homes. We need to add value to the digital highway we built. For this, we need to have a strong innovation team that will be anticipating the technology in the future and will maximize the infrastructure that we have—that's what I'm focusing on. Second, I want to make the Philippines a digital hub. Little by little, I plan to put up a huge development outside Metro Manila, a strong hyperscale data centre and to house digital content in the Philippines to serve our communities easier.

On Converge becoming a public company amid a pandemic

With the $250,000,000 investment, we built up more capability, because now we have the resources. Because without infrastructure, it's a chicken and egg thing—without the points how you can sell the lines, right? We forecast a roadmap for up to 2025: our target is 55 per cent of households by 2025, or around 15,000,000 or 16,000,000 home networks for which we are going to prepare the fiber line to be able to serve these households. That's where our roadmap came in. So, when initially the funds came in, we started focusing the rollout on Luzon, but that money isn't enough. That's the reason we went public.

Before you go public, you make sure everything is in place. You need to prepare your books, operations, network design, regulatory compliance, because once you become a public company, you should be ready for transparency. People were shocked when suddenly during the pandemic, with the stock market falling and everything, we suddenly came out with one of the highest Initial Public Offerings (IPOs) in the country. We generated close to another $500,000,000 plus dollars.

Even without a pandemic, we would still have been successful because broadband is now necessary especially in the Philippines. The average age is only twenty-six; 60 per cent of our population is young. We have 70,000,000 Facebook users. I understand we have 11,000,000 Filipinos working overseas, and these people are striving to send money to their loved ones in the Philippines to make their lives better. These Filipinos, when we didn't have the technology, used their money just to call and check on the families. Now because of the internet, they don't want to just call any more; they want to see their families through video. They want unlimited internet access. Not only that, but we also have one of the biggest outsourcing industries in the world and this needs the right infrastructure. They need to have a stable connection to be able to deliver the job right.

On today's young entrepreneurs

They are totally different. Unlike us, young people now do not have enough patience because they grew up with everything at their fingertips. But, I tell you, they are talented and they can be top for our economic development. They are really, really talented people because they grew up tech-savvy already. Now, our country needs to import more opportunities. We need to put proper infrastructure and proper working environments for this young generation because once they graduate, they will get bored, and where will they go? That's why they think of going abroad.

Fast Talk with John

What makes you Filipino?

I grew up here; I grew up in a society with the Filipinos. In fact, I took myself to court to get naturalized and it's very seldom people do that. The reason why I selected the Philippines is because I saw a lot of potential. We have this country and, I tell you, we are so lucky. We have so many natural resources. We have the best beaches in the world, we have the best agriculture, natural gas, and fishery. So, imagine how rich the Philippines is, and with so many talented people.

Is there anything from your country that you would like the world to know about or discover?

That the Philippines is one lucky country. We're in the middle of Asia. Imagine Singapore, Indonesia, Vietnam—if their internet traffic is going to the US, they need to pass the Pacific Ocean in our waters. The opportunity in this country in due time is for us to become the digital hub of Asia. But we need to address our cost; it's very expensive. Tax incentives are not there. Imagine, power—why should our power be so expensive? We have hydro, geothermal, solar, wind; it's about time we do something to disrupt the technology, the power setup. In due time, that will benefit the whole country.

If you could give a commencement speech (if you haven't already), what message would you want to impart?

Focus on what your passion is and choose your specialization. Are you happy with what you're doing? Then focus on that and you will become successful.

What would your epitaph say?

What's important for me is not the money but my impact on the community. I want to make sure that I have a good legacy that people will remember.

If there is anything specific you do that you would recommend I try, what would it be?

Having that love of country; it is very important. Culture is very important; love our country first. If you have that passion, I think that will boil down to the country's success and everyone's success.

My Thoughts

My fascination with Dennis Anthony Uy began when I actually got to know him as a person and got to know his story. I've always known his company, Converge—we are a customer at our headquarters, Dragon's Nest—but never really knew much about its founder.

When I invited Dennis to be one of our investor-judges on our reality show, *The Final Pitch* on CNN Philippines, he readily agreed, seeing our show as a way to not just find startups to potentially invest in, but use our show as a platform to get his advocacies known to more people. His story is the stuff movies are made of, and it just astounds me that someone who migrated to the Philippines as a kid, without resources and connections, can rise one day to become one of the most successful businessmen in the country.

Along with his *The Final Pitch Season 7* co-investor-judge Jay Villarante, we invested in one of the startups. The startup is Kintab, a mobile cleaning business poised to expand across the country. What excites me most about the investment is the prospect of working with Dennis as a business partner. I'll be looking to learn from his decision-making process, his speed and use of both reason and intuition in making business decisions, something that I was able to get a glimpse of during our filming of the show.

Chapter Assignments

If you're an entrepreneur stuck on your next business idea, take inspiration from Dennis Uy, who made it a point to follow where the industry's trends led him, while ensuring the fact that he always served the needs of his customers. To further help you zone in on your next big idea, try these exercises:

- Study your community. Look around; understand what their needs and pain points are. Listen to their sentiments—and see how you can create a unique solution for them. Personally talk to your current or potential customers. The wealth of insights will be so much deeper than relying on just your gut instincts and research.
- If you want to go big, start small. If you are looking at a particular sector or space, it would make sense to start an enterprise that serves the particular market. You will find that engaging with your market at any capacity can lead you to serving bigger needs down the road.

Kenichi 'Kent' Yoshida

Chief Business Officer
SoftBank Robotics Group

'We need to be creative. We need to be sometimes crazy for the business, but we also need to be realistic. We need to be both.'

Don't just look at technology or product—start with your customer

Since its founding, the SoftBank Group has believed that technology is key to building a happier and more fulfilling future for all. They see themselves as "Vision Capitalists", investing in human progress by building an ecosystem of entrepreneurial companies with new technologies and business models that will usher in an age of unlimited potential, fueled by massive improvements in computer processing power and memory.'

One of the great minds behind the organization is chief business officer of the SoftBank Robotics Group, Kenichi 'Kent' Yoshida.

For the past twelve years, Kent has been instrumental in the growth of SoftBank and has sat at the helm of various projects for new business development.

One of his best-known contributions is the launch of Pepper, the world's first social humanoid robot that has the impressive feature of being able to recognize human faces and read emotions.

That ability to lead such developments comes as no surprise as prior to joining SoftBank, he was the founder and CEO of the enterprise knowledge management software company RealCom, which successfully listed on the Market of High Growth and Emerging Stocks or MOTHERS at the Tokyo Stock Exchange 2007.

In this chapter, we have the opportunity to learn how Kent is able to steer the SoftBank Robotics Group in the right direction in terms of business innovation, and what it takes to succeed in the highly competitive and fast-paced world of technology.

On working with SoftBank chairman and CEO Masayoshi Son (Masa)

It's very tough to work with him, but we understand that this is the only way to survive in the IT industry. With the changing landscape every day or even every minute, that changes the decisions that we make. That is the culture of SoftBank.

In the words of Masa, we need to think through until the brains break up. We need to be creative. We need to be sometimes crazy for the business, to be aggressive to gain market share in a short time. Yes, we also need to be realistic. We need both. So, say, Masa has the last say, but I have to report, sorry, it's a good idea, but the reality is this, it's too early or it's too big to invest. That's the kind of decision-making process we have at SoftBank.

On robotics and automation technology

We started the business in the cleaning or facility management industry. We identify the target market we should go for. At the same time, we see the technological aspect. Say, five years later, autonomous driving will come. In our understanding it is not yet ready because for the safety data we need to be 99.999999 per cent for the public road traffic. However, indoor navigation is much more simple because there's no legal regulation and it's just low speed.

The technical readiness is different. For indoor mobility, it's already here, but outdoor low-speed navigation may be available next year and outdoor high-speed navigation about five years later. We need to see the market opportunity and the technical readiness.

That's the reason we have the two business units, SoftBank Vision Fund and, SoftBank Robotics. Before going into the big investment, we propose the solution to the client and if the customer says yes, we propose a proof of concept project and validate the technical readiness as well as the customer's needs. If the proof of concept is successful, then we can go to the investment. We can call it technical due diligence, but for us it's more like a proof of concept project with a real customer.

On Pepper, the humanoid robot

Pepper, the humanoid robot, is Masa's vision for the robot from around seven years ago. It can understand what people are saying and it can speak. There is a tablet on the chest, so that it can describe the information through its voice as well as the tablet. Several restaurants have been using Pepper for customer interaction.

Pepper started from hardware, with a vision, and the initial market was business-to-consumer (B2C). And we learned it's not a good story for hardware. It might be good for the software, but not for the hardware. There is huge investment for the manufacturing line and product design. So, we started from that market. That's why we started the SoftBank Vision Fund and Robotics. That's why we changed the target market from B2C to business-to-business (B2B). Pepper is still used at restaurants or hotels, but the important thing is how flexibly we can change the business model and understand the limitations of the technology.

Very important to remember in the robotics industry that, we shouldn't just look at the technology or hardware or product. We should start from the customer.

The effect of COVID-19 on the industry

COVID-19 is a big trigger for industry change. Before the pandemic, we had defined specs and it's not changed for thirty years. Now, we can look into, say, an invisible virus or scientific measurement over the air, floor, and use tests to count the number of microorganisms on the surface. That kind of a trend is a huge challenge for the cleaning industry.

The professional cleaning robot uses autonomous driving technology so it won't bump into a wall or hit people. Hopefully in the future, all of the tasks can be done by robots, but human capability is very advanced. I feel that it's very difficult to create a robot to do the tasks in the household. At least with the technology available at this moment, it can just do one part of the janitorial work. That means collaboration with the human janitor is still very important. It's not like everything is done by robots and machines. Human beings can manage a robot and sensor for let's say, low value added tasks. Then we can ask the janitor to upskill their capability so that they can be hygiene consultants or robot managers instead. It's not stealing human jobs, but pushing people to upskill and change their way of working.

On SoftBank's expansion across Asia Pacific

Currently, we do business in several countries including Japan, Hong Kong, Singapore, but we'd like to expand this business to all over Asia. We are going to launch in Thailand and Taiwan. We are providing digital transformation services, enterprise level support, as well as customer success consultancy.

On challenges, failures, and getting back up

When we do business, usually about 70 per cent of the new ideas become failures. So, in SoftBank Group, failure is fine, but we need to minimize the failure rate. The important thing is that we shouldn't die when we fail. We can fail, but we shouldn't go bankrupt or die. We can manage the worst-case scenario.

Fast Talk with John

What makes you Asian or particularly what makes you Japanese?

I'm a Japanese person living in Singapore right now. The difference between Japan and other countries is that Japanese education focuses more on how to estimate but we need to work on our understanding of how others feel. The Japanese people are good at understanding, but we are not so good at explaining.

I know you're living in Singapore now but is there anything from Japan that you would recommend for people to try?

Please come to Japan because Japan's natural and historical environment is really good to see. The food is also amazing and cheap, like beef on rice or gyudon.

Who is your modern-day hero, and if you have one, what powers would this superhero have?

My favourite quote is, 'the best way to predict the future is to invent it', which are the words of Alan Kay, the father of the computer. Apple Computer, invented by Steve Jobs, or Tesla Motors by Elon Musk. So maybe them.

If you were given a chance to give a commencement speech, what would be your message to graduating students now being thrust into the world? For those who are looking at possibly inventing the future?

Following the words from Alan Kay, we can say the same, 'the best way to predict the future is to invent it'. So please, do what you want. Design what you like to do. There is no limitation or restriction for the future.

What keeps you up at night or is there anything that wakes you up in the morning?

The business projects I'm doing right now are very exciting and that's the reason why I do what I do.

What is the one thing that you wish you could have known or learned sooner?

We are in the process of still developing with the market and focusing more on the customer adaptation or uses.

Outside of work, is there anything that you do in your downtime to regain focus?

Jogging or climbing a mountain.

We will all pass from this world. What would your epitaph state?

I don't want to have regrets or anything, so let's say: no regrets, because he tried everything.

If there's one thing that you do that you would for me or for anyone to try, what would that be?

Okay. I'm kind of a bookworm. So, I read a lot. I truly recommend that they read many books, science books like neuroscience or science of emotions, history, or business books.

My Thoughts

Much too often, entrepreneurs tend to fall in love with the solution without first totally understanding the problem or the market. For Softbank, it was the humanoid robot, Pepper. Pepper was Masa's vision for the humanoid robot years ago, which they later found to be the wrong way to approach the market.

I, too, have been in similar situations where I was just so enamored with the idea of starting a business, without first having intimate knowledge of the market and customer and what it is they really need. Hindsight is indeed 20/20, and I always chalk up these failed businesses or ideas to experience.

There are a few exceptions though, such as Steve Jobs who famously said, 'Some people say, "Give the customers what they want." But that's not my approach. Our job is to figure out what they're going to want before they do. I think Henry Ford once said, "If I'd asked customers what they wanted, they would have told me, 'a faster horse!'" People don't know what they want until you show it to them. That's why I never rely on market research. Our task is to read things that are not yet on the page.'

As a visionary myself, I tend to subscribe to Steve Jobs' way of thinking, though experience and failures have softened me up to consider a modicum of research before I pursue a major direction or path. I think it helps to have a healthy balance of both, if only to give more credence to a direction dictated by more than a hunch or gut instinct.

Chapter Assignments

As a Japanese working in the robotics industry in Singapore, Kent is exposed to the latest cutting-edge technologies, as well as different kinds of cultures. In doing so, he has gained a wide spectrum of knowledge that helps him as he develops solutions to address people's needs. You too, can take a page from Kent's book. Instead of diving headfirst into any random pursuit, consider the following:

- Before pursuing a new business or product, try to first gain firsthand knowledge, insight, even expertise into the industry. As soon as you feel you have enough information, try to see how you can come up with a crazy solution or business model that can potentially be a game changer in that sector. As Picasso once said, 'Learn the rules like a pro, so you can break them like an artist.'

- Widen your reading selections and learn more. If you're into fiction, grab books about science, history, business, politics, and so on. You will never know what inspiration will hit you when you intersect different worlds.

Dov Moran

Managing Partner, Grove Ventures
Serial Tech Entrepreneur and Inventor of the USB memory stick

'You can believe that you can go to the beach and lay down and look
at the sun and get an amazing idea, but it doesn't really happen like
that. If you want to be innovative, if you want to bring in a unique
idea, then be an expert in a very, very specific area.'

To find the best solution, connect the dots

*Dov Moran is one of the world's most prominent leaders in the high-tech industry, and
rightly so—after all, his invention, the USB memory stick, has become a global standard
solution for digital storage.*

This Israeli engineer and businessman embodies his country's innovative culture with over forty patents to his name. He founded M-Systems in 1989, which was able to grow its revenue to $1 billion, before eventually being acquired by SanDisk Corporation for $1.6 billion in 2006. This ranks as one of the biggest acquisitions in the history of business in Israel.

Dov is now passing on the torch to younger entrepreneurs by investing in very well-known startups as he is the managing partner of Grove Ventures, a VC fund with a quarter of a billion dollars under its management across two funds. Grove Ventures invests in leading startups that are developing hard-to-replicate solutions at the intersection of technology, science, and applicable market needs, including cloud platforms, big data, internet of things, digital health and more.

Dov is also the author of 100 Doors: An Introduction to Entrepreneurship, *where he shares his own experiences as a businessman in the high-tech industry.*

On his biggest childhood influence that developed his entrepreneurial drive

My grandfather was a great turning point. He had many international activities, but he lost everything in the Second World War. He had seven children; my father was the only one who survived. He lost his wife, he lost his property, he lost his leg as well. He was a very happy person, he was active, but somehow, he lost the drive to make money. All his life, I lived with him in the same home, and he always gave me missions, always gave me challenges, always made sure that I would be interested in mathematics and engineering. I see it is part of me today, being educated by a grandfather who had actually dedicated himself to make me whatever I am today.

I remember when I was a child, my grandfather found this house near our home, which was expected to be destroyed. He looked at the house and said, hey, all the shades in this house are relatively new. In our house, all the shades were very, very old, and it was the same size—so we basically made a project. We took all the shades from this house, four floors, moved them to our house, which had four floors as well, and he made an arrangement with the guy who actually was planning to destroy the house, and said, we'll do the project for you. And he said, *we're* going to do it. It's very difficult because these shades came with a piece of metal; it was very, very heavy, and you had to make sure that it wouldn't jump out when you're removing it. It is a very, very difficult job for a child of thirteen years old, and I do remember myself standing there on the fourth floor saying, 'I'm going to fail.' And he's standing there below saying, 'Don't drop it, stay still.' I looked at him and he said, 'Stay still.' Okay—I didn't talk, I went down, and everything was okay. Even today, when I am in very, very tough situations, and we are all in tough situations from time to time, I still have that picture of my grandfather standing, saying, don't drop it; stay still. Everything's going to be okay.

On entrepreneurship in the high-tech industry

When we think about high-tech and innovation, we always have the view that it is great, and everything goes perfectly, and there are great success stories. The way to success is to plan it—but with it comes many, many failures, and disappointments and difficulties. It's never easy as it sounds. In between the years 2001 and 2006, we had amazing, great success. We grew the revenue of the company from $45,000,000 in 2001 to over a billion dollars in 2006. This was a very, very unique experience, in general, for any company. It is very similar to the goals of Google or Facebook, when they go to the $1 billion level. And it seems like everything was great—but no, what you didn't see is that every quarter there was a disaster. So even when you are successful, and you are smoothly going from A to B to C to D, what you actually need to face all your life as an entrepreneur, as a CEO of the company, is struggle. That is the reality. So many times, when I speak to entrepreneurs, I say, guys it's great that you want to be entrepreneurs, it is great that you believe in yourself. You have to love what you're going to do—but that's not enough. You have to understand that you are going to a place where there are a lot of uncertainties, difficulties, and before jumping to this area, ask yourself: are you ready for all the difficulties that will come?

On entrepreneurs being born—and made

You know when they are evaluating winners in the Olympics, there's always the question of whether they are born winners or if they got there because of practice. The answer is that it's always a combination. Somebody who was born talented won't be number one, won't get in the Olympics if he does not work very hard and practice a lot to become the winner.

So, I am a combination as well, but let me explain to you something about entrepreneurship that most people don't understand, especially when they are asked this question—and I talk generally about the Jewish nation and entrepreneurship in general: everybody talks about Israeli startup relations, and that there's a lot of entrepreneurial spirit in this country. And that's true. You go everywhere—the number of startups, the capital, the work done in universities—and it's amazing, really amazing, but how come? Let me tell you a secret: Jews are not smarter than any other nation. However, I think that Jews are goal-oriented entrepreneurs, because 2,000 years ago they had all these problems, struggles, no ability to buy land wherever they were. They had no rights to buy land and to become farmers, and this is what most of the population actually used to be—farmers. So how do you survive? Many times, the government ignored Jews; how do people survive? And the answer is that the known entrepreneurs did not survive; they died. There are no entrepreneurs that survived. And this generation after generation after generation—over 2,000 years, the Jews who were left have become the ones who are truly the dependable entrepreneurs. It's not an Israeli tradition or function; this is a Jewish function or capability. If you look at America, many of the entrepreneurs in Silicon Valley are Jews. The population of Jews in America is less than 6 per cent; among the entrepreneurs in Silicon Valley, the numbers are so much higher, maybe four out of six: Mark Zuckerberg, the guys from Google, just to name a few. So, my answer: yes, it is in the DNA.

On how an entrepreneurial mindset helped his family survive the Holocaust

Let me tell you how my grandfather survived Holocaust: he had seven kids, two of whom were unmarried. They had factories of silver and oil fields, and he established a bank. When Hitler invaded Poland, my grandfather, the entrepreneur, said 'Hey, this guy's going to kill us. We need to get away.' He took his two children, the unmarried ones, and his wife, packed whatever he could and moved to Russia very, very early, before Hitler reached the city. I remember him telling me that he went to his neighbors and he said, 'Guys, we need to leave because this guy is going to kill us.' And they said, 'No, we just bought new furniture; if we run, the other Jewish guys would come and take everything we have. So how can we leave?' An entrepreneur always looks at the risks, not only the vision, not only the dream; when it is required, it needs to pivot. My grandfather, an entrepreneur, understood the threat that was coming. He had probably made plans, but he said, hey if I stay, I die. I need to change. He lost his property. He lost his other kids as well, but at least he and my father survived—so I'm here because of my grandfather.

On his learnings from serving in the Navy

I went into the Navy, and I studied engineering; my father was an engineer as well. And when I went to the Navy, into the microprocessors department, and now these were the days that microprocessors were something new. It was very exciting because this was pioneering, and then you get to be a commander at a very, very early stage. So, I had a team that worked for me, and I had many, many projects. And, in general, since these are all young people, you have the responsibility and soil to innovate, to come up with ideas. I became the commander of the microprocessor department at the age of twenty-six or twenty-seven; that's a very, very young age, because when you go to a real-life factory, you would become an engineer, or a senior engineer when you are over forty. And when I got out of the Navy, I was very well-experienced. I had a lot of self-confidence—maybe too much self-confidence. I said, 'hey, I'm not going to join other companies', I established my own company. That's the benefit of going to the Navy, and in general, Israel is a country which is surrounded by enemies, which are much much louder, and in order to survive, in order to do whatever we need to do, we have to be sophisticated, otherwise we're going to be washed off. Therefore, the Navy, the Air Force, and Intelligence are quite sophisticated, and that allows us to keep the balance between us and our neighbours.

On Dov's invention of the USB

In general, when you are in the Navy or service, many, many times, you're facing situations that are telling you: hey, there's a problem; solve it. You have to find a way to connect the dots. It changes, somehow, the way you think about issues. You are structured to be innovative, not just to take things as they are. And this is very important when you are an entrepreneur because the whole idea of entrepreneurship is not to copy somebody else or to do something that others did already, but to come up with things that are very new, come up with things that are disruptive, these ideas that others did not have the ability to seek or were not smart enough to think about at the right time.

In the case of the USB flash drive: I went to New York for a conference, and before a conference, I always open my computer. I go over the presentation, change a few things here and there, and that's what I did during the flight. This was twenty years ago, and computers were not as good as they are today. I got to New York in the morning, went to the conference, and it was my time to give the speech. I went to the stage, opened my computer, and nothing—the computer was dead. Two hundred people in the audience, all are looking at you, waiting for you to talk. You have a scheduled time. And the question is, what do you do? You may tell me, okay, talk without the presentation. That's easy. You can speak without the presentation. But those days, I was much younger, much less fluent. And when you are a public company wherein your presentation includes a lot of data, all this data needs to be very accurate. You can't make a mistake in the data.

So, while standing, there's that feeling of sweat on your back. So, I was startled, and while I'm standing there, one of my friends said, 'Hey, take my computer.' But how could I transfer my presentation for my computer to his computer? Meanwhile, I hooked my computer to the power, and it came back to life. I gave the presentation, and when I finished the presentation— and I still remember this exact moment—I took off all the cables. I said to myself, never again in my life am I going to give a presentation without having a copy in my pocket. The whole idea was, I want to have a copy of the presentation in my pocket. And then the question was how to do it. Now, I knew what flash was, and we did some projects related to speed—and by connecting the dots, you get this idea to make a flash drive. That's the story. It's very simple.

On coming up with the next best invention

You can believe that you can go to the beach and lay down and look at the sun and get an amazing idea. But it doesn't really happen like that. If you want to be innovative, if you want to bring in a unique idea, first of all, you need to study. Be an expert in a very, very specific area. And then you can come up with an idea which will really take the universe, take civilization one step forward.

Steve Jobs didn't finish college, but Steve Jobs was somebody who, all his life, was studying and studying. He was the face of discipline, and he never stopped studying and understanding. His level of understanding in computers was very, very high. His company was fifteen and a half years old when I invested in him. Today, it's the largest company worldwide. These are the outliers. We can't beat the outliers; we can't try to be the second Steve Jobs. I studied, and I went to Technion. It was difficult. I did my first degree. I studied for my second degree. And when I meet people, I see the big difference between people who studied and really understand very well.

There are shortcuts to success—but don't rely on shortcuts. You can go and buy a lottery ticket and win; every day there's a winner, but instead of trying to buy lots of tickets, it's better to go study and build something, and trust your capabilities rather than your luck. That's the point.

On his personal mission today and working with young entrepreneurs

What guides me today? I want to make this world better. Now, I want to be successful in venture capital. We do invest only in companies that are making a big focus on the world. We don't invest in companies that do advertisements to just generate money. I want to see companies that are bringing unique value, unique products that are actually working to enable faster communication, better computerization, larger storage—making this world smarter.

I still work very, very hard. I think there are very few people who are working harder than me. I actually work around the clock. I go to sleep every day at two in the morning. I don't go on long vacations. Almost all my time is dedicated towards my job, but I see my mission and I enjoy very, very much what I'm doing. Again, I am a very lucky guy because, actually, my work is my hobby. I am blessed by the fact that I can see amazing entrepreneurs, young people, smart, very unique, and very innovative. I get to see the inventions, things that are going to change the future, and that makes me very happy.

On seeing the impact of his invention of the USB flash drive

I remember I went on a flight, and then someone approached me, someone whom I had never ever met before. And he said, 'You invented this USB flash drive?' This was maybe three months after we launched the product. So very, very new people talk about the product. I said, 'Yes, I did. I'm implementing systems.' He said, 'You won't understand it, but I want to thank you because you saved my marriage.'

He goes on to say, 'I'm working in a place which is very, very demanding, and I cannot not take my job home. And I have two young kids. My wife is always complaining that they never see me come home before they go to sleep, and I can't come home earlier because I have a lot of work to do. I'm not allowed to take this data out of the place. So now, I can just copy that data, go home early, be with my small kids, then go back to the computer to complete my job. Come back the next day in the morning, plug the USB in, copy everything. Everybody's happy. My wife is happy. The kids are happy. My boss is very, very happy.'

When I spoke with this guy, I said, 'Wow, I didn't know that this is so important.' And this may be the first. And I remember, the whole flight, I had a smile on my face.

Fast Talk with John

What makes you Israeli?

I'm a Jew first. My parents came here, telling me all my life that this is the land of the Jews. We have to fight for that. We have to keep it like that. I think that Israelis are very well-connected to one another, compared to other nationals. And that's me, that's some part of it. We are not afraid of failure. Israel is a place where it is very difficult to manage people because everybody believes they are smarter than others. You are not going to tell me what to do. I tell you what to do. And that's the mentality. I am part of it—the good stuff, the bad stuff.

If you could give a commencement speech (if you haven't already), what message would you want to impart?

First of all, we are living in a world that is changing very, very fast; a world where everything is computerized. Everything is big data, artificial intelligence. Many new jobs will be created that don't exist today. And you need to stick to that. You want to be in the new world, rather than being in the old world. You need to study, understand computers, understand physics, understand medicine, understand the body, nature. Be very curious in order to constantly learn and improve yourself.

How do you prepare for what you do? Any special routines you can share?

I walk, on a regular day, 15,000 steps, 25,000, or even more. I try to stick to my diet and I'm a vegetarian. I don't touch meat or fish. My target is not to slow down or do worse. My target is to do well.

I do have a rule. Except for interviews like this, where I need to stay in one place, I never talk on the phone while sitting. I talk a lot on the phone during the day. I do at least a couple of hours overall of talking. So, while I'm talking, I'm walking, and I walk very fast. So, I walk out of the office. To other people, normally I'm the walking guy.

My Thoughts

To actually meet a person who has invented something as ubiquitous as the USB flash drive is quite a trip. You would expect that the guy would be somewhat of an outlier genius with superhuman gifts of intelligence and luck. The more I talked to Dov, the more I realized the facts of what he says are actually true. Most people who come up with these world-changing innovations are no different from you and I, but they really are the product of hard work and seeing things that others don't.

I also love the fact that Dov only invests in companies with unique products or those that bring unique value. This is something I've also kept as a guiding principle for all my business endeavours. I've always found fulfillment in the creation of a business or company that creates something new that is of value in the world.

I am fortunate that I've had similar experiences of being approached by people telling me of how something I created had made a profound impact on an aspect of their lives. My first book, the self-published *Project: First Home: Everything you need to build your house from scratch*, birthed a lot of home build and sell entrepreneurs or contractors who used the book as a guide to help them start their business. Our show *The Final Pitch* has also inspired many aspiring startups to try their hand at entrepreneurship, with the goal of creating their own tech companies and also possibly one day pitching their startups on the show. It's a very rewarding feeling to know that what you do actually has made an impact on the lives of people and contributes to the creation of more enterprises and jobs.

Dov advises people to be an expert in a very specific area. 'And then you can come up with an idea which will really take the universe, take civilization one step forward.' At different points in my business life, from having zero knowledge in the industries that I entered, I was able to give value to the real estate industry as well as the world of startups and investing. This did not come overnight but was the product of years of finding the right opportunities and working hard to learn as much as I could about the industries that I entered. It also took a lot of guts to accept that I did not know anything, that I would make a lot of mistakes, and that those mistakes could be the seeds for a future innovation that I may or may not find. Regardless, I made sure I put in the work and saw for myself where things lead.

Chapter Assignments

Dov shares with us two seemingly contradictory but also very wise practices—in tough situations, to stay still, and to always keep moving. Try both in the context of your daily work:

- When going through an issue at the office, avoid reacting right away to the problem. Breathe in, stay still, and then focus on the best solution at hand.
- Do what Dov and many other experts recommend to avoid being sedentary at work: get up and walk around every twenty minutes. It'll help your eyes get a rest from all the screen time too. Better yet, take all your non-video calls while walking. String together an hour for calls and take them outside or anywhere you can safely walk without being interrupted.
- What can you potentially be the expert—and possibly even be best in the world—at? Exercise your creative thinking and look at the problems you would like to solve. Do you have a personal pet peeve that can turn into an exciting opportunity for a product, service or business? Make a list and see what problem or opportunity you are in a unique position to help solve or take on. Then, gather the resources and skill sets to put yourself in a position to do it.

Jose Magsaysay Jr.

Potato Corner
Co-founder, CEO, and chairman emeritus

**'If you find your specialty and mastery, you will grow.
You just don't realize it but you will explode.'**

Focus on one thing

Jose Magsaysay or 'Jomag', a former janitor and employee, launched with his partners a flavoured French fries food cart business called Potato Corner with P 150,000 in 1992.

Since then, over the last thirty years, he has expanded his business not just in the Philippines but also abroad and declared more than a billion pesos in dividends.

Coming from the Magsaysay political and business clans, he's a nephew of former President Ramon Magsaysay.

Before launching Potato Corner, he had been in the food business, working with Wendy's for about a decade. He also had a stint with Mister Donut.

He's had five brain surgeries, but nothing's stopping him from bringing Potato Corner to even greater heights.

Below are excerpts from my interview with him on the Methods to Greatness podcast.

On focusing and mastering the game

It was me with only one choice, no lifelines. It was just Potato Corner. I had to make sure that all my effort and everything I did was for Potato Corner because if it failed, I had nothing. There was no friend to call, no bank deposit somewhere that I could live for if the business failed. I had no choice but to make Potato Corner successful.

I think what helped Potato Corner was our ultra-focus and mastery on a niche and that was the micro-F&B. We decided, let's just stick to being a micro or cart operator because we are the most experienced cart operator probably in the world and especially in the Philippines. We have the capability of creating our own benchmarks, our own rules, and best practices in this industry. Let's just be the best micro cart operator in the country or in the world. I think that's our advantage. We made sure we stuck to this and not get attracted or sidetracked to another business. Although a lot of people think the cart business is like a second-class citizen, to us it's not. It's our bread and butter, it's our livelihood, it's our profession, it's our specialty. I think if you find your specialty and mastery, you will grow. You just don't realize it, but you will explode.

By understanding the business very well, you're able to play the game and you can influence the result of what's happening. Us in franchising, because we study it very well, we are able to influence the result of the games we play. In fact, benchmarks and rules are just our baseline.

We create our own micro best practices in this industry, that's how important focus and mastery in the game is. You're able to create your own rules. And for rules that you cannot change, for example, because of the government, because of taxes, sometimes you're able to skirt in and out of the rules. You know how far you can get out and when to get back in. If there is something I can share with everybody is, first master the game you're in and focus on that one thing only.

I think it's also a question of morality and conflicts. For example, when I was running Potato Corner, I was in no other businesses but Potato Corner.

When I joined Mister Donut, no other business, not even helping Potato Corner, just Mister Donut. When I came back to Potato Corner it was just Potato Corner and nothing else. When I became an investor, only an investor. Now I don't even try to meddle in management or put up my own business and run it on my own. Like when you're driving, 100 per cent of your IQ is driving, you can see what's going to happen, you can anticipate a lot of things. When you pick up your phone and start texting, 50 per cent of your IQ is now driving, 50 per cent of your IQ is now texting. Sometimes you don't end up where you're going, and you don't know how you got there.

People keep on saying, oh it's good to multitask, but remember you multitask only the things that you take for granted. The most important thing: never multitask. Put 100 per cent of your IQ and focus on one thing. Taking care of a crisis is all about anticipation, but if you're not 100 per cent in the driver's seat, you will not be able to anticipate future crises, problems, and opportunities.

On working with business partners

Potato Corner became successful because I realized how hard it is to start a business on your own. The four of us did everything together so that I could focus on one thing, one could focus on one thing, and that I think was the secret recipe. It was just making sure everything became cohesive at the end of the day. But that's the hardest part to do. But the best thing to have with partners is making sure that everybody has a designated job.

We learned after two years it wasn't good to be all bosses. Our vision was all the same, but we have different ways of getting there. So, we got an outside party and we told that outside party, 'Can you chair the company for us and tell us what to do and teach us how to separate being friends and being business partners?' That person came in and told us what to do.

If you look at the history of Potato Corner, we've always sought help from outside parties. Our heads of departments, business units, operations, franchise, logistics, were run by managing consultants. We're always looking for help outside and I think that also made the difference why we were able to grow rapidly.

On keeping the company lean

We run everything ourselves. I was delivering french fries, I learned how to carry three boxes, one on each shoulder and then one somewhere somehow,

I don't remember. We kept the company very lean all throughout. That's the reason we survived the Asian economic crisis. We never borrowed and, if you look at our business model, we franchise. Because you franchise, you use other people's money to grow instead of borrowing to put up our own stores. We used franchising to grow and because of that, we were able to leap from one store to seventy stores in two years.

Adjust your organization based on the need to grow. For example, Potato Corner has been only scaling up its support services in its offices. If you're getting fat and your pants are getting hard to close, that's the only time, for example, we expand. We add people, we increase the office size, we increase the storage sizes only when it's about to explode or to burst in the seams. We never adjust our organization for expected or future development. We're very careful about that.

I've seen so many businesses who, because performance is good now, invest in other facilities, bigger offices, or add more people because they expect more sales to come in. But sometimes it doesn't always happen. This COVID-19 crisis is a good example. Nobody expected sales to halt or stores to close, so if you build your store based on expected sales, then you're in trouble.

On franchising

The moment a person asks you for a franchise you better be prepared to say yes. The person who asked you that question already likes your product. It means that they like your business model. They're not stupid. They ask you for a franchise because they know they will make a profit. They know it will be successful. But if you say no to them, there's a potential that they would put up their own business like yours, or you just created your own future monsters.

What Potato Corner did, we let go. Somebody asked for a franchise, yes, you have a good site, yes. So let it go. I understand a lot of people are not like me who like to franchise, like to share the business. There are not too many people who enjoy talking to other partners or to a franchisee who will tell them, I don't like this, can you change this, can you use this product. Because a franchisee is also an entrepreneur, they will tell you what they like, what they don't like. But if you're thinking about becoming a dominant factor, if you're thinking of being worth billions in the future, then market dominance and hyper growth is a good path on achieving that.

I think momentum is brought by not stopping, but by always being open to new things that are coming your way. It's not about money. It's about just saying yes to somebody's proposing something or maybe seeing what will happen ten steps away.

On being the perceived first mover

By the second year there were more than 300 who copied flavoured french fries. But because we franchised, we cemented our foothold on being the dominant brand and the perceived first mover. Is the first mover advantage important? It's not always because if you are the first mover and you don't expand rapidly, whoever expands rapidly faster than you becomes the perceived first mover and will have that first mover advantage. Market dominance is about rapid growth.

On taking care of franchisees

It definitely is not about franchise fees or growing right away. It's about taking care of your franchisees. The most important thing to us is taking care of our franchisees, watching and always worrying about their bottom line. We didn't sell them a franchise and forget about their bottom line. Every day that's all we think about, the bottom line, and the performance and the happiness of our franchisees, and the return. If you notice our franchise fee is almost the same as the fees that we charged twenty years ago. It's because we're always thinking about the return or the payback of our franchisees, because we always think about the long-term. We want the soonest payback. It's better for all of us and our business would become long term.

On continuous learning

I was a college dropout because I had to work. I think being a dropout made me work harder because I had to prove I was better than some graduates. When I had the chance to go to graduate school and take my master's degree in entrepreneurship, I think that helped our company because I now had the confidence after the Masters in Entrepreneurship (ME) programme to take the company to the next level. I think going to school and graduating during a time of crisis is very important. I encourage all of you to study during times of crises since everything slowed down anyway, maybe everybody will have time to study. I'm trying to enroll myself now in a PhD in Data Science because everybody now knows how important data and technology are.

On psychotherapy

I have no complaints; life is good. I had a talk with my sons, and I apologized to them. I'm with my wife Inez almost every day now and we're together all the time. You know what helped? Four years of psychotherapy. If I knew psychotherapy would help me, I would have it done to me maybe like thirty years ago. I didn't realize my childhood issues would affect my life today, so I'm glad I took psychotherapy. I think everybody should try psychotherapy. Nobody's perfect and I think all of us have childhood issues because our parents are not perfect also.

It didn't only help me, therapy also helped, I think, the whole company because I became aware of my shortcomings.

Fast Talk with John

What makes you Filipino?

My name. Magsaysay means to talk, to tell a story. It is a Tagalog word from the word *saysay*.

If you were given a chance to influence anyone from outside the Philippines, what is the one thing that you would like for that person to see, taste, or discover about your home country?

It's our love for family. I think one of our biggest assets is how close we are with the family. I think that that speaks about how we love each other. The other thing is service. I think what the Filipinos and what the Philippines should be known for is how we serve the kind of service we do globally. In fact, if you remove the Philippines out of the equation from service around the world, I think you'll have a different kind of world. Filipinos, our nurses, our managers, our teachers are doing a good job running the entire world. Our nannies, our housemates, they are heroes. I think the Philippines should realize that and promote our heroes and not look down on our domestic helpers, our overseas workers who are going out of the Philippines. That's the way we conquer the world, by conquering every service industry. We can be the world dominator in service if we just set our minds to it.

Is there any person out there who you feel is your hero or who would be in your opinion a modern-day hero?

Well, the Filipino overseas workers are still my heroes. I'm proud of them.

If you could give a commencement speech, what would be your advice to the graduating class who are going to come into this world?

My advice would be to look for a good therapist, a psychotherapist, talk about your childhood issues, find your strengths and what your purpose is because the sooner you find your purpose—sometimes it takes a lifetime—you are ready, you have your own guiding light. A lot of people have to find another guiding light to steer them but if you can find your own guiding light as soon as you can, especially if you're fresh graduates, by getting a psychotherapist maybe to help you find what you're good at, what your purpose in life is, then you're all set in life.

What keeps you up at night and, in the same breath, what gets you up in the morning? Is there anything that is troubling you with all the success that you've had and is there still something that you'd like to achieve?

I just want to help startups or new entrepreneurs or other entrepreneurs who I enjoy mentoring. I enjoy coaching of course; I learned that from our gurus because of what and how they coached me. I'm just giving back on that part now. As far as what I need, I don't need anything any more. In fact, I realized that I'm very simple and it's actually the things out there that made me want some of the things that I didn't have, that I didn't need. I sold my Mercedes, my Jaguars, my other cars, my other motorcycles that I really love because I don't need them. I just realized you have to grow up. Part of my growing up is, 'that's enough, been there, done that, five brain surgeries, stop dirt biking' or something. I finally realized that I have to grow up, so I love riding my scooter now.

What do you do in your down time?

I ride around almost every day on my Honda Beat. I take the scooter's trail, also I ride the scooter dirt biking.

Is there anything you know now that you wish you could have known sooner?

No, I have no regrets. I'm probably where I am because I worked harder because I wasn't a graduate. Potato Corner is better because I took the ME programme. If I were to go back in time, I'd take psychotherapy earlier and not wait until I'm in my fifties. I would have had a better life with my family, people at work, and my partners.

What would your epitaph say?

'A good father and a good husband.' That's enough for me.

Is there anything that you could recommend that I try? I think I already know the answer to that question so I think I will take you up on your advice to seek psychotherapy.

Have you heard about the third option? The first option is staying married, the second option is separating or divorcing, the third option is fixing and making your relationship better. If Monica and you are interested, I can refer you to a friend who brought in this third option programme to the Philippines. It enhances marriage, it's like a mastery of getting married. It did wonders for Inez and me. In a nutshell, this is what it is: we cannot change our partner; we can only change ourselves.

My Thoughts

When I interviewed Jomag for *Methods to Greatness*, two things stood out for me. The first is his penchant for focusing on just one thing. The other is his revelation on psychotherapy being integral not just to his personal and family life but also to his business. The former is something I myself have always believed to be true. One can never really be a jack of all trades and master of all. The latter is something that, to that point, I had yet to explore.

Jomag was one of the first investor-judges on our business reality show *The Final Pitch*. A year after his debut on the show, he was diagnosed with a serious brain condition, which necessitated a number of brain surgeries through the years. I've always known of his battles with his brain, but never with his mind. I would later realize that all of us, no matter how successful (or sometimes because we *are* successful), are always going through something that people are not aware of.

Through the years that I've known Jomag, one advice sticks out: since you can't do everything by yourself, find partners who complement your weaknesses so that you can focus on your strengths. When I first started my business in my mid-twenties, I was too focused on becoming a solopreneur—not onboarding partners because I wanted total, complete control of the business without having to answer to anyone but myself. My growth as a businessman and as a person happened when my partner, Monica, who eventually became my wife, joined me in the business. Though I must admit that working with your significant other poses many challenges. In my case, it was one of the best things that could have happened to me business-wise. And as we grow our organization, we are now looking at involving more people who can share in the responsibility and fruits of growing the businesses to a much larger scale.

Chapter Assignments

Jomag's story is a testament to his determination and resilience. Along the way, he has armed himself with knowledge and guidance from experts. How can you find your own method to seek mentorship and guidance?

- Continue learning—not just by earning post-graduate degrees. Learning can come in different forms. Taking art or language classes, trying a new sport, or even going to a new country and staying for a week or a month.
- If you're putting up a new business, find partners who complement your strengths and support your weaknesses. If you are a visionary, find someone who is good at operations or finance. If you are the technical person, find a partner with the entrepreneurial propensity and marketing savvy to get your product to market. Always build a team that is well-rounded so you get to cover all bases.
- Working out our deep-seated issues through psychotherapy can help us live more meaningful and fruitful lives. Find one you trust and respect, and it can work wonders for every aspect of your life.

Jessica Chen

Keynote Speaker, Emmy Award-Winning Communications Expert
Founder and CEO, Soulcast Media
Top LinkedIn Communications Instructor

**'Communication is what you say, your body language,
and your tone. People only think it's usually the first one
but really, it's the marriage between these three.'**

Communicate and storytell your way to success

*Jessica Chen is a trusted communications advisor to several tech leaders in Silicon Valley
and in Asia. With a degree in International Studies and experience as a news reporter,
she founded and sits as CEO of Soulcast Media, a business communications agency that
provides high-touch strategies to elevate people's public communications skills.*

Chen won an Emmy Award for Television for her extensive coverage of wildfire in California. As business reporter at Time Warner Cable, she placed first for Best Feature Story awarded by the Associated Press.

Chen is one of LinkedIn Learning's top instructors where her communications courses have garnered more than 1,000,000 views.

On languages

I am American-Chinese. However, my background is Chinese and I say that in a way where it is my first language. Despite being born and raised in California, my parents definitely instilled in me that speaking Mandarin was going to be a very valuable skill. Fortunately, I know how to speak Mandarin Chinese. Obviously, here in California, I speak English because a lot of my clients speak English but I work with a lot of people in Asia as well. Because English is a global language, too, we can communicate in both depending on what people are most comfortable in.

On becoming a journalist

I didn't even study journalism in university. I studied International Business, so when I decided to become a journalist, I realized that I had a very hard long past to really prove myself in terms of my capabilities. I started out like a lot of young people. It's all about getting that experience, and internships. That helped bolster my resume and I always say that the first job sometimes is the hardest job to get. But once you are in it, it's much easier to rise up from there.

So, my first job in the US was actually at NBC in Reno, Nevada, which is a few hours away from Las Vegas. I started there then I moved to New York City. That was probably one of the best experiences. Working in a really huge, fast-paced city and, at the time, I was probably in my early to mid-twenties. That was a really good experience. I moved to ABC in San Diego, California.

On winning an Emmy award

I think for those in the media, winning an Emmy is one of those coveted awards that kind of solidifies the work and the effort that you put in. I was with ABC10 in California then. It's every journalist's dream to win an award like that. That award showcased what it's like working in the media industry. I think it highlighted a lot of the communication and presentation skills that I had to also learn to hone to such a degree, that it was recognized. I'm really grateful now because a lot of the things I teach are things that I learned on the job: how do you become a better public speaker, how can you be more convincing, how can you use storytelling just like you imagined.

The story that I ended up covering was a huge wildfire that happened in San Diego. Typically, in a situation like that, you might be familiar that it's breaking news, right? You're talking about evacuation, safety, and what the firefighters are doing. From a journalist's perspective, once this breaking news happens, it's boots to the ground; you're going towards the fire, you're covering it and I have to say it wasn't just my effort. It really was a team effort. We have a group of journalist producers who are really coordinating all this. The coverage that we did was I guess to a point where we did it all really well, we executed it really well, we were able to find the good stories. I'm very proud to have won an award like that but obviously not for a situation that affected a lot of people.

On building confidence

One of the reasons why I started Soulcast Media was because I myself was not naturally confident or even a good communicator, in my opinion. That journey to build confidence isn't easy. In the work that I do at Soulcast Media, I also talk a lot about linking cultural elements for why it was such a struggle for communication. I've identified myself with eastern principles because we are taught things like humility and respect. These are principles that are absolutely so important, but it doesn't necessarily give you that confidence to advocate for yourself, which is so critical at work or if you're pitching a new idea.

I feel like the work I do now I can empathize so well with entrepreneurs, executives, and business owners who want to talk about themselves but they're not necessarily comfortable. For me, my whole philosophy with Soulcast Media is how do you find this balance. How can you still advocate for yourself but not necessarily show off or boast because nobody really likes it anyway, right? That's kind of the premise of Soulcast Media where we teach people how they can speak better, how they can engage with people, how they can really be thoughtful in their approach.

On presentation skills

When it comes to presenting or pitching your idea, your energy level on camera is so important because if you cannot show excitement about your own product, about your own service or whatever it is, how can you expect other people to be excited about it? You always have to be mindful of your energy and how you're showing up, which goes into the tone of voice, right? A lot of people, when they speak, they kind of speak in this very monotonous voice and that's just not very interesting for people to listen to, and that's a fact. When we talk about variety, it's talking about speeding up, slowing down, going high, going low, and choosing which words you want to emphasize. When you get to that word, and you hit that word, then you slow down. That's a lot of the work that I do when I work with entrepreneurs; a lot of times entrepreneurs they want to start with a script. And that's fine, we can start with the script; that'll allow us to pull out the most important parts. But now, once we've pulled it out, how can you make sure that when you are delivering the message it's making the biggest impact? Because, again, words are important but how you deliver it, honestly, is even more important.

On being among LinkedIn's top instructors

LinkedIn is one of my favourite social media platforms and, in this day and age, there's so many to choose from. For me, strategically, I chose LinkedIn as my platform because the work that I do and the work that I want to do are with people who are in the business industry. Where better can you find those people than on LinkedIn? I feel that the people on LinkedIn, when you engage with them, are a lot more professional. They're there because they care about their career, and they want career advancement. I knew that LinkedIn had this audience that I was targeting. That's business. From there, what did I do? My expertise is communicating on camera so I just started posting these videos of me sharing communication tips that I thought could really help people.

LinkedIn saw these videos. They liked my background as a broadcast journalist, and then they invited me to become one of their instructors. The first course I ever created with them was teaching people how to develop an executive presence on camera. When COVID happened, people's desire to learn this went up. I've created five more courses with LinkedIn—all communications-related. Now, I have a total of six courses, and I have over a million views on these. I just am very proud to be able to share my skills with people who just want to learn how to be better. I'm just happy that there's this resource now for them.

On working with entrepreneurs for their pitch

I love working with entrepreneurs, specifically on their pitch deck because they, first of all, are so hardworking. They have this brilliant idea and they're already starting to work on this idea. But they always will reach a point where they're like, 'Oh my gosh I need finances and I need to talk to investors.' How do you fill this gap?

What I've noticed is a lot of these entrepreneurs, even though they are so brilliant, they just cannot necessarily express that enthusiasm to people who they really need to sell this idea. I worked with people who are just raising, like a few hundred thousand dollars to over $500,000,000 dollars and obviously at that point they're already in Series C, Series D.[5] But the nerves are still there, and it will never go away.

When I started working with those kinds of entrepreneurs in the later seed round investment, obviously their companies were a lot more established. But, again, there are still new things that they need to talk about; there are still new ideas they need to get investors excited about. When I work with them, and this is probably pretty universal, when I work with people on their pitch deck, I always focus on the first five minutes of their pitch deck because that is when you have to capture their attention. If you cannot capture their attention early on, you lose them. It's much harder to gain it back in the middle of your pitch. Do we talk about things like what's the most interesting part of your company? Start with that and not only start with that how can you say it so that they're like wow that's impressive. Obviously, this looks different for different companies depending on what it is that they're pitching, But I would say every entrepreneur needs to focus on the first few minutes of their pitch deck pulling out the most amazing, impressive parts and start with that.

If you don't have a track record to show for it, what really is going to sell is how passionate you are about this idea. Because early on, in any company, especially if it's just an idea you know there's not much backing or necessarily validating this yet, what investors are investing in is you; you as a person. Obviously, the idea has to sound pretty good but, in the end, they're investing in what they see in you: your passion, your drive, your enthusiasm because they want to know that when things go bad are you going to get out of bed the next day and still work on it. I think early on whether it's

---

[5] Series C and Series D are the one of the last few stages in startup financing before an IPO.

somebody who's a teenager or somebody who's in their mid-twenties who wants to start their idea and they're starting to work on it. It's really about showcasing that passion that'll get people to get excited with you. That's the most important.

On how to become a good communicator (post-pandemic)

One of the most important things about how anybody can be a very good communicator is really thinking about other people first. I know that isn't necessarily a tactical skill, but I truly feel that the most powerful communicators are very mindful of the people in the audience; what is it that they care about and speaking to them and being as helpful as they can be. Because one of the things that can instantly turn people off in any situation is when you just kind of continue to talk about yourself and it just seems very self-serving. But if you can be of service to those who you're speaking with, whether it's your team, just one person or a group of people, if they can see how valuable you are, suddenly in their eyes they're going to think 'Wow, Jessica or John, they're really able to contribute.'

I think it's always being mindful of your audience, making sure that you know and think about what they care about and this is where preparation is really important. As you're preparing for your next five o'clock or three o'clock meeting, think about who's in this meeting, what are we trying to accomplish here, what do I need to bring to the table and then how can I communicate this so that it resonates with people.

On storytelling

Right now, I'm working with an entrepreneur. She's creating her pitch deck to share with investors and her struggle—and perhaps this is a struggle with a lot of entrepreneurs—is about the way she talks about herself and her company. She talks like she would just read credentials like a resume. I did this, I did this, I went here, I did that. Nothing about that is very inspiring. Impressive, but it's not very inspiring. When I started working with her, we had to really talk about how everything kind of connects and that's really the storytelling part of it. How did you get from A to B to C and how did you fit into this picture? So, for her, as I said, the first few minutes are the most important. I had her introduce herself, I had her introduce her company. But what was most impressive about it is that she has had successful companies in the past, one of which is valued at half a billion dollars. That is impressive! But what did she do? She buried the lead. She should have started with that. This is how she could have built her credibility. She talks about who she is and how she's already built a successful company because it's already valued at $500,000,000 dollars. For her, we didn't really change her background. You can't really change someone's background, but you can change how you tell it. That's the most important.

Jessica's Tips on Communications

1. **Don't undervalue how important it is to carry yourself when you're speaking on camera.**

   A lot of times, especially again with the beginning of COVID everyone's like, 'Oh yeah I get to work from home, I get to wear my pajamas.' But I still think that impressions are always being made. Even though you've worked with your team for many, many years, trust me; they're still looking at what kind of backgrounds are going on, what it is you're wearing. So, putting even just a little bit of effort can really help.

2. **Know how to carry yourself.**

   Little bits of effort on how you carry yourself can make a huge difference now when it comes to communication. Communication is what you say, your body language, and your tone. People only think it's usually the first one but, really, it's the marriage between these three so when I communicate, especially on video, because there's a barrier, there's a distance between you and me. I try to make sure that I'm incorporating body language as much as I can. I'm using variety in my voice because that's how you build engagement.

Fast Talk with John

What makes you Asian? Or, specifically, what makes you Chinese or Chinese American?

It's always a really funny question because I don't think so much about it. I feel that my natural way of thinking is naturally very Asian. What do I mean by that? I think, just in general, the way I think is again leaning more towards Asian, eastern principles than western. But because we live in a western world, you really have to adapt and challenge yourself. Going back to talking about things like humility and respect, I think, for me, I find those things extremely important.

I live in a western society, so I always have to remind myself that advocating, communicating, or expressing myself is actually also quite important. To answer your question, I think my beliefs and the way I think are already very eastern because that's just what I was taught growing up.

What is it about China that you would like for people to know or for those who would like to understand China better?

There's a reason why people are saying that this is truly the next superpower country. The rate of growth, the rate and speed of the type of innovation production that's coming out of there are truly unprecedented. As technology grows and the thing is it's because countries like China, one of their biggest assets are they have just a lot of people, they have that manpower to really get things going. Perhaps I'm biased but I think—this is a huge generalization—Chinese people are very efficient. They want to get things done. They work fast, they want to accomplish things and I feel like that speed in which they work can be a huge asset combining it with making sure that everything is right and accurate to avoid mistakes. I think China or Asia, in general, is really kind of where people need to open their eyes to.

Who, to you, is a modern-day superhero or who is your modern-day superhero?

People who just get things done, honestly, you're a superhero. You just get things done and you don't try to be super loud about it. That's a superpower sometimes too.

If you would be given the privilege of giving a commencement speech, particularly now, there are a lot of students who are coming into the world with uncertainty, what would be your advice to those students?

Back to even when I was graduating from university, what was something that I wish that I had tackled earlier on . . . For me, and maybe this is because I'm just a little biased, I would say learn how to be a very good communicator. The earlier you learn how to do this, the easier it'll be for you to fast track your career. Get noticed and communicate your thoughts. There is a difference between communicating with your friends and family and communicating with those at work and in business. It's different and the reason is because when you're with your family and friends, you can be a little bit more relaxed, you can just be a little bit more comfortable. Invest and learn how to be a better communicator. If you do that when you are young, I truly think that this is what differentiates people. People who stay stagnant versus those who rise up more quickly.

My Thoughts

Jessica being Chinese American straddles the dichotomy of the East and West both in her career and the expectations foisted upon her depending on the society she's forced to navigate at any given time. Work and career dictate for her to be more adapted to a western society, but it is clear that it is her upbringing and eastern lineage that ultimately informs her decisions on a daily basis.

It's surprising how much it reminds me of how we Filipinos also have a unique perspective in that we are Asians, yet our history of being colonized by the US makes us equally open and accessible to Western culture and sensibilities. The fact that a good number of US call centres are based in the Philippines is a strong testament to how good Filipinos are at communicating. Our excellent grasp of the English language and western culture, coupled with the innate Filipino traits of warmth and hospitality make us a natural choice.

Yet I struggle with the reality that, although call centres are the low hanging fruit that brings in much needed revenue to our country, the fact remains that Filipinos who work in call centres are still employed—as opposed to putting up and owning their own enterprises. Most Filipinos are taught to be good employees, and not necessarily good entrepreneurs; something which has been part of my personal mission to help change.

On a separate note, being a former news producer and reporter, I also relate to Jessica and how this particular career path uniquely prepares one to be an outstanding communicator, regardless of how much experience, confidence, or predisposition one may have to telling stories. The first advice that my first boss in TV news gave me was for me to get in front of the camera as much as I can. A stand-upper is the term for when a presenter gets in front of and speaks directly to the camera. I was already a decent writer, but incorporating my own voice and personality, placed either as bookends or at critical parts of a story, gave the storytelling a whole different meaning and perspective. Your tone and opinion, sometimes even just showing yourself having fun, can create the moment that humanizes the piece and brings it to a place that people do not just understand and relate to, but remember. The advice to get in front of the camera as often as I can helps me to this day when most of us are in front of cameras on a daily basis. In this day and age, a successfully told story or pitch can be attributed as much to the virtual messenger as it is to the message.

Chapter Assignments

Public speaking and communicating is something that many people are afraid of doing, or afraid of doing wrong. Jessica's training as a journalist allowed her to perfect the craft. Whether you are a student, an employee or a businessperson, you have to ace the art of communication.

- Start working on your communications skills by taking classes or practicing with peers. Try to find a workshop or class you can attend that will allow you to hone your public speaking skills in front of a live audience. Your future Ted Talking you will thank you for it.
- Give equal importance to written communication. Vanessa Van Edwards of Science of People recommends balancing both warmth and competence in composing emails. I recommend you look her up and apply your learnings in the next email you compose.
- It may be something that just makes you cringe but do take a video of yourself speaking, whether alone or in front of an audience. Nothing beats instant feedback, and you will realize things about your manner of speaking, standing, hand gestures (or lack thereof) that can come from simply recording yourself and watching yourself speak.

Minh Bui

Rising multi-industry serial entrepreneur
Beta Group founder and CEO

'Do you connect with that business idea or the customers at the heart level? Do you love the solution that you're trying to provide for them? Do you care deeply about the impact that your product or service could have on your customers?'

What can I do for my customers?

Minh Bui, also known as Minh Beta, is an entrepreneur from Vietnam with a passion for social impact and creativity.

Bui Quang Minh graduated from Sydney University in 2006 under the AusAID scholarship programme. He later earned a Fulbright scholarship and his MBA degree from Harvard Business School in 2014.

Minh started his first business—a chain of donut stores—when he was twenty-five, selling it in 2012 before leaving Vietnam to attend Harvard University. Returning to Vietnam in 2014, he founded Beta Cinemas, a chain of affordable cinemas.

His company has since evolved into the Beta Group, of which he is founder and CEO. Minh Bui has businesses that include a startup called A.Plus Home, a network of affordable serviced apartments for the youth, and Crimson Business Institute, which offers Harvard-licensed courses in business education for Vietnamese learners.

Active in music and the entertainment industry, he has also engaged in various film and art projects.

On growing up in Hanoi

When I think about my time growing up in Hanoi, I think it was very local. Because I lived on the outskirts of the city, I didn't really meet a lot of foreigners and my everyday life was very, very routine; it was very quiet and peaceful. But at the same time, I observed how my parents were always trying to make something more for their lives. They always tried to work on a business venture, trying to train staff to be better employees, thinking about a new product to launch in the market. They were small business owners, but they were always hustling. I think I got a lot of that work ethic from them and also the inspiration that I picked up from observing the way that they create a life that they want us, their children, to have.

They were basically just trying to earn money from the different small business ideas that they may have. My mom would at some point try to make rice wine to sell to the neighbourhood, or she would have a small business buying and selling scrap metals. I think the solution-oriented mindset is something I inherited from my parents.

I was always studying and trying to be a good student because I saw how hard my parents work. I got into the best schools in Hanoi and into this new environment where a lot of smart, enthusiastic, and very dedicated students are my friends. They are always talking about some thing like moving to America or the UK to study and so that sort of sparked in me this curiosity about the outside world. So, I started to look into different options, and I wanted to go to America for my bachelor's degree, but my parents really couldn't afford it at that time. This amazing scholarship programme came to my attention from the Australian government. It was a dream come true and I tried to apply for it, and I got in. It opened so many doors for me from that point on.

On new learnings and developing a critical mind

As a student from Vietnam, you are supposed to listen to what the teachers say and think of that as the ultimate truth. But when I went to Sydney University, the teaching method is different; the mentality, the mindset is very different. They encourage critical thinking. For the first time, I thought it was okay to think differently, to be entertaining weird thoughts and different ideas, and testing different kinds of options. That was very exciting for me because I have this tendency to want to be creative about things. When I got that opportunity to be able to think creatively, I embraced it and until now I try to live my life that way.

On changing mindsets and amplifying impact

A lot of times, when people think about business in Vietnam, there's a general idea that this is greedy; it's viewed in a negative sense. So, what I'm trying to do and sort of convince the public is that business, when done right, could generate profound impact. I came up with this term, 'amplifying impact'; basically whatever we do we try to provide customers with products and services that are satisfying but also would change them in a way that would allow them to go on to be different people and continue to generate that positive impact in whatever they do. For example, with my Crimson Institute, I license content from Harvard and use the case method to teach business and leadership, and what I have been seeing is that my students become better leaders. So, the transaction stops after they finish the programme, but it doesn't stop there; they go on to become better leaders, they become more empathetic, they become more loving, they have more kindness for their team.

On immersing himself in his chosen business

After eating a donut in Singapore, I wanted to bring that to Vietnam. I also think I saw that as an opportunity to foray into business. I got a job working in the kitchen, learning to be a baker because I didn't know how to make donuts and that was something very new even in Vietnam; like nobody knows what donuts mean. I went back to Vietnam, I invested all my savings into the first store, and I just keep pushing myself to learn more about the business and try to be better. After three years, we got to six stores across the country, so it was quite a success because people were so excited about something that was so different. The way that I designed the store is very different, the way that I put up the colours and all the things that I observed from the retail shops in Singapore, I tried to incorporate that in the first store in Vietnam.

On making decisions and starting anew

When I reached six locations, I started to struggle with the road ahead. I didn't know how to continue because I was not a great manager, I tried to do everything by myself, I spread myself too thin, I don't trust people, I don't build on people. I didn't know how to. Even though the business at that point was still making some decent amount of money, I sold the stores to different buyers. I didn't even know that I could package and sell the business. Then I applied for my MBA because for me education is something that I knew that I want to pursue for my whole life because I realize the profound impact that education would have on me as a person.

I had some money after finishing my MBA, so I used that fund to start the next venture which is the cinema chain. I looked at different options and accidentally saw the news about CJ Group buying MegaStar.[6] So MegaStar, at that point in Vietnam, had seven locations and it was sold to CJ, which is the Korean group, and they bought out the business for the valuation of almost $100,000,000 for only seven locations. That would cost about like maybe $10,000,000 max to set up; so for me that was like, why would they pay so much for it? I went deeper into it and did my research, and I was like, okay the cinema market in Vietnam is very nascent, very early, and it's a good business, good margins, and the execution is not that different from the way that I did my donut store, just a little bit bigger and a bit more complex but I can understand the process. I was also very passionate about the media industry. I'm a creative person, I write songs, I like music, I sing, I also did some acting as well. It was a perfect opportunity for me and so I went ahead with that.

---

[6] MegaStar or MegaStar Media Company is Vietnam's leading cinema chain.

It was fun but it was also very tough because we had to compete with a lot of the big players in the market. We were very small; we didn't have a lot of money. I only had like $250,000 and it takes at least about a million to set up a cinema, so we had to go to a smaller province. I had to select an affordable strategy because that strategy made sense and fit perfectly within my budget. Also, because I understand how the income of Vietnamese people is not super high, not everyone can afford a very expensive movie ticket. I think that is thanks to me growing up on the outskirts of Hanoi. I was hanging out with people who are conscious about spending, struggling with their daily needs.

We started with one location and then we got funded by some international funds. After five years of running Beta Cinemas, I started feeling like I didn't have an opportunity to have as much impact as I could for the business itself. When you get to like fourteen locations and opening another location, it's just another problem that is the same that I already trained my team to do very well. I have a Chief Operating Officer who's always been with me since day one, and he's basically a better operator than I am to be very honest.

I have been looking for other opportunities and technology is something that I have always been thinking that I need to embrace because that will allow me to optimize my impact. During my time at Beta Cinemas, I also got to understand my core customer segment very well. Those are young people who are mostly migrants from small provinces to big cities. A lot of them struggle with the living conditions because they are renting, and the rental market in Vietnam is so fragmented, unorganized, and poorly managed.

On thinking about customers' needs

The idea for A.Plus came about when I think about the skills that I already have for Beta Cinemas combined with technology. The idea for A.Plus came from just that one thought: what can I do for my customers, for the people that I come to interact with and understand the pains of? The living condition is something that they struggle with and that is one of the most fundamental problems that anyone could have.

The idea for Beta Cinemas, for example, it's not just about providing movie experience to people who didn't have access to it before. It's about giving them the sense that their life is now better, that they can go to enjoy something 'luxurious', something that, before, only people of a certain class could enjoy. At A.Plus, we understand how if a person feels good about themselves, feels good about the place that they live in, they would go on to be confident members of society and grow into their full potential. In our location of A.Plus, for example, even though the price is very affordable, we make sure that they have clean water, we make sure that the environment is clean and nice, the neighbours are safe and decent people, and we also want to provide them with educational services.

I would say in selecting businesses it's not so much about us trying to figure out which opportunities are there but it's more about, within my horizon, within what I can see and what I can do, which one is the most profound impact that I can generate for those people? It comes from a place of care, it comes from a place of love, and I realize that that is the only reason that would keep me stuck with anything.

On selecting businesses to go into

I wouldn't say there's so much as a process, it's more like a checklist now. That checklist could be: do we have the skill to execute this well? Do I deeply care about the customers that I'm serving and the value that I can bring for them? Can I scale this venture massively? What would be the factors that will stop me from scaling quickly?

You have to ask yourself: do you connect with that business idea or the customers at the heart level? Do you love the solution that you're trying to provide for them? Do you care deeply about the impact that your product or service could benefit your customers? Because if you're only chasing money or opportunistic ideas like benefits, it's not going to last, because it's very tough. So, the only power that can sustain you through is the deep, deep love that you have for that idea, for that customer segment, or the particular solution that you came up with.

Fast Talk with John

What would you say makes you distinctly Asian, particularly what makes you Vietnamese?

I think family values. I connect with my family in ways that's beyond reasoning. I think that is something very Vietnamese and also something very Asian. We care for our family members in ways that are hard to explain. There are things that we are willing to do for our family members that don't make sense sometimes but then we also fight and that's so difficult to explain.

Is there anything about Vietnam that you would like for people to know or discover?

A lot of people know about Halong Bay, it's very popular, but I would want people to try to go to Ninh Binh. Similar scenery but a bit different and more secluded. I think it's very beautiful, it's an area in northern Vietnam. This particular landscape complex is very scenic, like Sydney, and you can go in like a cave and see wonderful sky and green lake. The name is Trang An and the province is Ninh Binh.

Who to you is a modern-day superhero and what special power does this hero possess?

My superhero is my mom, because she's the most positive person that I've ever come across and she can always see the great, the good in people, and she always sees the good in any situation. That is something for me is very powerful because with that I think life is just going to be better.

Would you mind sharing with us the main message of a commencement speech that you've done?

The main message would be life doesn't matter that much. That sounds crazy but that is something that I realized after COVID. I actually got COVID for a few days; I got a fever so high I thought I was going to die and in those moments, I was ready to die. But after I recovered from it I have this new sense of freedom that life doesn't matter that much. The time that we have on earth is limited so why don't we just enjoy and do anything we want, live it fully, live to our full potential and not be afraid of anything that usually holds us back. It's usually not the way that we think it might turn out to be so go on and live life with bonus, with bravery, with courage and with kindness, because life doesn't matter that much.

Is there anything that keeps you up at night? Is there some big dream that you haven't quite accomplished or something that you would like to pursue that keeps you thinking or maybe gets you up in the morning?

Recently I have been doing a lot of meditation and, for some reason, that makes it hard for me to sleep. I don't know why but that is what I'm going through right now. I meditate a lot and I get very calm and relaxed the whole day. Before, I got stressed out easily so at the end of the day I got very tired, and I could go to sleep because of all the tiredness and the tension. But now

I have less of that so even at the end of the day I'm still very calm and relaxed and it's hard for me to go to sleep. I know it doesn't make a lot of sense. That is something interesting too because that means there's so much that I don't understand about my own inner world; that is something that I want to explore further.

How do you prepare for your day? Is there a particular way that you are able to focus on the things that you need to do?

The thing that I find most helpful now is actually starting my day with some meditation because I found that as I do that, I can set up my mind to be at the most calm and positive. If I start the day angry or mad usually the day would unfold in that direction as well.

If you were to pass, what would your epitaph say? Is there anything that you feel speaks to how you've lived your life and how you'd like to leave it?

I want to be known as the man whose impact would live on. I feel like we came into this life and we didn't have a lot; we came into this life with this physical mass that we are, and then from that point on everything generated from that is impact. So, whatever I do right now is about maximizing the impact and I hope that when I pass that impact will live on.

Is there anything specific that you would like for people to try, whether it's something in your business or your personal life that's worked out for you?

I gave up coffee recently and it has been doing wonderful transformations for me. For the past ten years, I drank coffee maybe two to three times a day. During COVID time, I bought an espresso machine and I just kept making coffee with that and drank like three or four every day. I got very anxious and almost depressed, and I didn't know why because I'm usually not experiencing those issues. Coffee is the only reason I could pin it to, so I stopped. In the days that I stopped drinking coffee, I had massive headaches and kept craving for it but then it eventually passed. I got into this mentality of being so calm, tranquil, and clear. I realized I had been addicted to coffee for the last ten years without even knowing it, without realizing the full impact that it has on my body and my sleep pattern and my psychology. So, to anyone who is drinking coffee heavily, I think they should try to give it up for a few months and see how they change.

My Thoughts

I could not help but relate to Minh's stories of how his parents, who were small business owners, would have unending small hustles—anything that would be a good idea to generate income. My parents were the same. When their tailoring business went under in the eighties, they tried to stay afloat by getting into other things such as flea markets and bazaars. I remember as kids how we would go with them as they sold their wares—everything from undergarments, T-shirts, headbands, and soft drinks.

Growing up in a very entrepreneurial household, my parents, despite not having the regularity and safety net of a nine to five, were nevertheless happy and content with their businesses. They were able to send us children to good schools, and more importantly at least for me, it gave me the notion that entrepreneurship, though risky, is a path that is worth taking.

Minh's entrepreneurial endeavours—from donuts to cinemas to schools—at face value typify the opportunistic drive of a serial entrepreneur. There seems to be no rhyme or reason to his choice of industries. But only through interviewing the founder do you realize that his decisions and direction come from a deep understanding of his strengths, and how he can use this to be of service to people. His guiding principles, his 'why', arm him with the energy to fuel his pursuits.

My own serial entrepreneurial journey—from TV shows to real estate to startup enabling—follow a similar trajectory that comes from knowing my strengths, and being guided by my desire to help my fellow entrepreneurs participate in nation building.

Finally, Minh's studies abroad were the catalyst that fueled his next entrepreneurial moves. My own graduate studies when I took my ME at the Ateneo de Manila, and the executive programme of Singularity University in Silicon Valley that I took ten years after that, were responsible for opening my eyes to other possibilities I would not have imagined had I remained in the bubble of my own thoughts and goals. There is so much one can learn not just from our professors and gurus, but from our classmates and peers that can catapult our way of thinking. For my own master's degree, I remember that the business I was able to generate just amongst my classmates was more than enough return on my investment of time and money to enter the programme.

Minh's Harvard experience has inspired me to put on my bucket list a similar goal of one day taking the Harvard Owner/President Management (OPM) programme, delivered in three units that span twenty-four months over three calendar years. Learning has always been an exciting and soul enriching exercise for me, and I truly believe that this is something that I will continue doing long after my entrepreneurial itch has abated.

Chapter Assignments

Minh Bui is a proud Vietnamese who's making a name for himself as a serial entrepreneur. With his learnings in his own country and abroad, he hopes to contribute and create a meaningful impact in others' lives. Here are some things you can try:

- Study abroad. Whether it's for college, for a master's degree or even a certificate course. Studying abroad will allow you to broaden your horizons and allow you to see things from a totally different perspective. I've done this with a one-week executive programme in Singularity University in Silicon Valley, and it was an eye-opening experience that gave me the blueprint for a business that we are putting up.
- Looking for a few ideas on what business to put up? Start with yourself and what you're good at. You will find that there are certain things you do and do well that people may want to also learn or be more proficient at. Come up with a list of your talents and skills and try to figure out which ones you can charge money for. Then put out an ad on social media. You have to start somewhere.
- Find inspiration from a trip abroad? Why not find a way to launch a similar product or service back home? In our highly globalized world, fusion is the name of the game. You will never know what newfangled discovery can be a hit in your neighbourhood or city.

James Soh

Founder, Renopedia

**'Do not take risks just for the sake of taking risks.
You must take calculated risks in life.'**

Be stubborn—but take calculated risks

*As the founder of Renopedia, Singapore's number one online portal for all things renovation,
James Soh is a millennial entrepreneur whose story is one for the books. Coming from an
underprivileged background, James' family migrated to Singapore from Malaysia when he
was only three years old in search of a better life. While his parents sacrificed a lot to put
him through school—and despite his best effort to honour their wishes—James dropped out
of university and pursued entrepreneurship instead.*

James actually had the opportunity to pursue either architecture or engineering at the National University of Singapore back when he was nineteen years old. However, after fulfilling his civic duty with the country's national service, James was introduced to the world of multilevel marketing (MLM), which got him thinking: what do I want to do with my life?

Given Singapore's economic situation back in 2005—there was a recession, university graduates couldn't find jobs, basic salary started from only $1,800, starkly different from today's $4,500—James decided to try his hand at making his fortune through MLM.

At age twenty-two, James found himself in $50,000 worth of debt. However, James admits that his stubborn nature wouldn't let him just give up, so he decided to open a small F&B business by taking out a loan.

At twenty-five years old, he was out of business, out of work, desperate—and virtually bankrupt. He still tried his hand in business, this time by taking a shortcut and opening a foreign domestic worker agency without paying the appropriate fees—something he eventually paid for dearly, and which led him to go back to the drawing board, again.

His saving grace was a job he landed with a publishing firm. That's when things started to turn around for James as he became the top sales executive at the company for three consecutive years.

When he was finally ready to establish his own venture again, James founded Renopedia, working hard to build a directory of over fifty interior designers and over 250 product vendors. Witnessing the start of the digital revolution, he invested heavily on digital and social media marketing to boost brand awareness.

Today, James is thirty-seven years old and oversees the newest, youngest, and fastest-growing online renovation media company in Singapore. From large interior design firms to small companies, he helps them take their digital advertising campaigns to the next level.

In 2021, in the midst of the pandemic, Renopedia made $3,000,000 in revenue.

His goal is to help companies thrive in the twenty-first century marketplace, ensuring that no business, big or small, gets left behind. The plan for Renopedia for the next three years is expansion throughout southeast Asia.

On his experience in MLM—the good and the bad

Let's talk about the good: when I came out of the national service, I used to be a person with very low self-esteem. One of the reasons I joined is also because, imagine, on my first day at the company, I saw a huge stage, and then—one of the oddest things—four people going up onstage to receive their cheque. They give speeches, and these people are only two, three years older than me. So, one thing about MLM: it builds your confidence. I was supposedly going to be a university student, so I was book smart; what I was lacking was street smarts. To get with people, to be able to understand how people work, how different people think, and talk to different levels of people. These are the things I learned in the MLM company, and also some sales skills because you need to sell. You need a lot of search engine optimization (SEO) strategy. And another thing is entrepreneurship, because you must understand that when you go to an MLM company, you are not a salaried person. You actually work for yourself.

For the bad—I won't say all MLM companies because that's unfair to judge all MLM companies. The company that I joined was a local company, not a multinational corporation, and, at the time seeing people at twenty-two years old, twenty-three years old driving cars, I was fascinated. But what we don't know is that these are all on the surface because these are people in Singapore buying cars, but they don't have enough money for their own expenses. They fake it to make it. One of the famous quotes that people like to say is that: 'If you are not a millionaire, act as if you're a millionaire, because you must have the mindset before you can become a millionaire.' So, people like me, I tend to be blinded by what I see. Another thing: the company I joined was a company with a lot of young people, so all of us tended to behave a little bit recklessly when it comes to decision-making. That's also one of the reasons that almost led me to bankruptcy at the age of twenty-two, twenty-three years old, but it's also a good thing because when I started to do business later, I did not just take risks for the sake of taking risks. You must take calculated risks in life.

On how he got himself out of debt

I just focused on work. From nine to six at the company I would focus on work, and even after six, I would still focus on work because I could not focus on other things. Once I focused on other things, I would see all the negative things that happened. Within one year, I managed to repay all my debts. In three years, I was promoted four times, all the way to senior business manager. I was hitting my sales target every single month, so I saw my salary growing and growing and growing.

On observing industry trends and getting ahead of changes

By the time I was twenty-nine years old, I started to realize that something was happening in Singapore. People were not reading magazines. There was a transition to digital with people looking for things more on Google, etc.

I started to see that my company was actually becoming part of a sunset industry, so I really had only two choices: one, I find another sales job; two, I try another business. But when you have bad experiences in the past, and you're young, when you share with people that your business has failed, they will say, 'hey, you're not cut out for business', including my parents. So, you better find a stable job. If you get yourself into more trouble, you will be a burden to your family; people around you will be stressed. But somehow, and maybe this is just my stubborn nature, I ended up starting up another business: a maid or foreign domestic worker agency.

In Singapore, if you have a maid agency, you have to apply for a license. So I went into this business, but somehow, and this was stupid, I wanted to start without paying the fees. So I actually operated the business illegally; I tried to do some recruitment without a license, and it was illegal. I was found out by Singapore authorities, so they invited me to their office and they temporarily allowed me to apply for a license.

Okay, so I was back to zero again. At that moment, I asked myself: what can I do? Mostly, I was thinking about advertising. In my previous company I was selling advertisement space for one of our interior design magazines. A lot of people have asked me how Renopedia started. It's not as if I had a mission to create the number one digital online renovation platform in Singapore. No, it was because I was just at that crossroad of my life. Everything just seemed to work out, so I tried it.

On expanding one's business to different countries

We are the first renovation platform company to look into the whole of southeast Asia because we realized that the Western renovation culture is focused a lot more on DIY. We set our target on the whole of southeast Asia, and now we are already starting in Malaysia. When expanding, we have to understand the culture first. We have to consider the fact that we are not just expanding our business; we are also integrating our whole company culture into that country's. It's also about: how am I going to build a team over there? What is the minimum salary of these people over there? And what is the salary package that I have to work out? Another thing we have to work out is also the purchasing power of consumers: how much are they willing to pay for renovation? We have to change our marketing strategy, too.

Fast Talk with John

What makes you Asian?

I will say that I'm an extremely fast-paced person—and I am somebody who is scared to lose, somebody who will always be eager to prove himself, somebody who wants to be someone.

Is there anything from your country that you would like the world to know about or discover?

Singapore is a very safe place.

If you could give a commencement speech what message would you want to impart?

Life gives you a lot of change, and these are all challenges for you to become a stronger person. A lot of people want success. They try to find success. But success is not a goal—it is a journey.

What gets you up in the morning?

It's definitely my passion for my business. When we first started, it was more about me building a platform, but now it's more than just a platform. It's the family culture within my company.

How do you prepare for what you do? Any special routines you can share?

The first thing that is important is your Monday, okay, because Monday is the start of the week. I will always have this Monday morning planned. After you do your planning, you realize that at the end of the day, you won't be rushing into things every single day of the week. I tend to plan on a weekly basis. Do I plan on a monthly basis? Definitely, that's more towards the start or end of the month.

What would your epitaph say?

I believe it will say something like: a strong man with strong views.

If there is anything specific you do that you would recommend I try, what would it be?

Try to be the better version of yourself by getting out of your comfort zone. Success is about proving something to people by breaking through yourself.

My Thoughts

That's really great advice; to me the way I see it, doing something that scares you, doing something that maybe you're not 100 per cent ready for, but something that you'd like to do that is really a leap of faith—that is something that may make a tremendous difference down the road.

I've personally taken on some things in my life that I did because I saw it as a challenge, even if I didn't have any clear idea how I could pull it off. Starting my TV and video production business from my bedroom at twenty-five, marrying my wife and starting a family at thirty-six, and expanding our business outside the country at forty-five. Sometimes you just have to put yourself in a situation where you have no choice but to make something work, and figure things out along the way.

Chapter Assignments

Join me on this one. I'll try to see what things I can get into that are outside my comfort zone, something new and that will push me beyond my boundaries. Feel free to change and improvise if you've done any of these before:

- Live in another country for two to three months. This is big for me considering I have a family and business in Manila. I'm sure we can make this work somehow.
- Expand the business to other countries. We are on the verge of doing this for our show *The Final Pitch*. Outside of the Philippines, we are expanding the show *The Final Pitch: Asean* to Singapore, Indonesia, Malaysia, Thailand, and Vietnam. Do you have a business that can potentially be expanded to other cities or locations, if not countries?
- Take the good points of MLM and see how this can be applied to your business.

My Mind Journey

One of the best results of me writing this book is that it has forced me to do or even prioritize things that I have been putting off. To begin with, I took Jose Magsaysay up on his suggestion to seek help and go to a psychotherapist. I knew that it was something I wanted to do eventually. What I didn't know is that I needed it sooner than I realized. Like a tumour that has metastasized, a problem is usually a manifestation of a much deeper psychological problem or trauma.

The process of seeking a psychotherapist is quite daunting. After all, you are essentially seeking someone who you will pour your heart, soul, and the deepest recesses of your mind to. The day I sought out one was the day that I admitted that I could no longer put things off. I needed a professional to help me make sense of what was happening in my life and why they were happening.

As a psychology undergraduate, I knew enough perhaps of human psychology to have a vague grasp of what I was and am going through. My fears of abandonment, caused in part by childhood trauma and early adulthood friends leaving the country, made me form a protective wall that made it hard for people to come in and for me to develop long lasting friendships.

But then the realizations from my first psychotherapy session made me realize things that I had lost and are now slowly unearthing. I had lost a part of myself, and I am now on a journey to find myself again.

I came to the realization immediately after my first session: 'why did I never do this before?'

When I was writing this, I had just finished my second session with my therapist. My therapist also recommended that I write my thoughts down in a journal. This is something that I felt I didn't need to do before, since I've always felt self-aware and in touch with my feelings and emotions. My therapist, however, pointed out the importance of keeping a record of my thoughts, having something to look back on that really examines my state of mind at a particular moment in time. Having this snapshot will enable me to realize perhaps at some point in the future of how far I've come. This will allow me to draw a mental map of who I am, who I'm not, and who I would like to become in the future.

Some people see me as a successful entrepreneur. I've been producing the long-running TV show *Philippine Realty TV*, which is now coming into its twentieth season. It's a show where I build concept homes from the ground up. Our family's dream home, a fully automated smart home, was built on our show. My other show—*The Final Pitch*—has made possible the investment of millions of dollars into the Philippine startup ecosystem and is now going global. I have always prided myself in my mind, and like the people I interviewed in this section on the mind, my ability to imagine a vision and make it come true. Despite all these successes and achievements, however, I sometimes feel that the impact of what I do is not enough, and that there is so much I have yet to do. I also oftentimes feel alone and isolated.

My therapist gave me a mental exercise I could try. 'Imagine you're all alone, naked, in a secluded beach or island with no one and nothing surrounding you. Without accolades, achievements, material possessions. A voice then asks you, "Who is John?" What would you say?'

I actually did not know how to answer the question, and it is something that I know I will have to journey to discover. I will have to work on myself first in this journey of self-discovery before I am able to see how my past has affected and continues to affect my relationships with the people in my life, and my future.

In my pursuit of my goals and what I believe is important, I have somehow lost myself in the process. I have to reconnect with myself again.

Act 1: Mind Key Takeaways

So, what are the common themes that I've found that stood out from this room of great minds? Failure, focus, and diversity of thought. Below are notable quotes that helps me to ponder on how to strengthen my mind:

Failure

'So, the idea is, how do you create a culture that not only encourages people to think for themselves, to not be afraid of making decisions, to learn from mistakes? If we want them to rely on themselves by making decisions, we need to provide them a setting where they can make mistakes; otherwise, they would be too afraid to decide.'

—Inbal Arieli

'When we do business, usually about 70 per cent of the new ideas become failures. So, in SoftBank Group, failure is fine, but we need to minimize the failure rate. The important thing is that we shouldn't die when we fail. We can fail, but we shouldn't go bankrupt or die. We can manage the worst-case scenario.'

—Kenichi 'Kent' Yoshida

'The company I joined was a company with a lot of young people, so all of us tended to behave a little bit recklessly when it comes to decision-making. That's also one of the reasons that almost led me to bankruptcy at the age of twenty-two, twenty-three years old, but it's also a good thing because when I started to do business later, I did not just take risks for the sake of taking risks. You must take calculated risks in life.'

—James Soh

Focus
'Focus on what your passion is and choose your specialization. Are you happy with what you're doing? Then focus on that, and you will become successful.'
—Dennis Anthony Uy

'I think what helped Potato Corner was our ultra-focus and mastery on a niche . . . We decided, let's just stick to being a micro or cart operator because we are the most experienced cart operator probably in the world and especially in the Philippines. We have the capability of creating our own benchmarks, our own rules, and best practices in this industry . . . We made sure we stuck to this and not get attracted or sidetracked to another business.'
—Jose Magsaysay Jr.

'Be an expert in a very, very specific area. And then you can come up with an idea which will really take the universe, take civilization one step forward.'
—Dov Moran

Diversity of Thought
'As a student from Vietnam, you are supposed to listen to what the teachers say and think of that as the ultimate truth. But when I went to Sydney University, the teaching method is different, the mentality, the mindset is very different. They encourage critical thinking. For the first time, I thought it was okay to think differently, to be entertaining weird thoughts and different ideas and testing different kinds of options . . . When I got that opportunity to be able to think creatively, I embraced it and until now I try to live my life that way.'
—Minh Bui

'I feel that my natural way of thinking is naturally very Asian. What do I mean by that? I think, just in general, the way I think is again leaning more towards Asian, eastern principles than western. But because we live in a western world, you really have to adapt and challenge yourself. Going back to talking about things like humility and respect, I think, for me, I find those things extremely important.'
—Jessica Chen

Intellectual humility is at the core of great minds. The acceptance that failure is part and parcel of success, that focusing on something and not believing that you can do everything shows wisdom in restraint, and that diversity of thought and acceptance of off-tangent views can help us expand our minds and ways of thinking.

In the next section, we transition to a journey of the body and, as you will see, the transition is not as clear-cut as one might imagine.

Act 2: Body

'Your body hears everything your mind says.'

—Naomi Judd

The connection of the mind and body is one that is inextricably linked.

As we transition from the mind to the body, this section on the body begins quite fittingly with Miss Universe Pia Wurtzbach as she shares with me equally as many insights about mental health as she does on body issues and, eventually, the power of body positivity.

Mixed martial artist heavyweight champion Brandon Vera gives me an honest assessment of being an athlete extending peak performance up to your forties, and how disastrous not being prepared can be.

Businessman-athlete Toby Claudio talks to me about the business of sports and how it has shaped him and his businesses, and how sports have changed the lives of poor communities in the Philippines.

Olympian pole vaulter EJ Obiena talks about overcoming a lackluster athletic career as a young student-athlete, breaking record after record when he got into his stride, and takes me through his mental and physical preparation that made him Asia's best pole vaulter in history.

Television host and brand ambassador Rovilson Fernandez talks about the physical rigour of a television and hosting career, staying fit and being in shape for the job, and being a Spartan race ambassador.

Medical entrepreneur Chien Han How talks about the importance of good quality sleep, new sleep technologies, and how to age better.

Finally, legendary basketball coach Chot Reyes shows us the blueprint of a successful athlete, life after sports, winning your mornings, and how to be a supportive parent to your athlete child.

Whether you are a young athlete, someone having body issues, or want to extend your peak performance as long as you can, this section on the body will hopefully help you power through your struggles and challenges.

Pia Wurtzbach

Miss Universe 2015
Co-host, Between Us Queens podcast

'We are not after perfection, but progress.'

Invest in yourself

In 2015, the world, led by beauty pageant fans, witnessed a real-life plot twist. The wrong candidate was accidentally crowned winner of the Miss Universe competition, leading to the dramatic reveal by embarrassed pageant host Steve Harvey of the real Queen: Pia Wurtzbach, the Philippines' representative. That moment, and the fact that Pia reclaimed the crown for her country after over four decades, cemented Pia's place in history.

Born in Germany to a Filipino mother and German father, Pia Alonzo Wurtzbach grew up in Northern Mindanao. At an early age, she became the family's main breadwinner after her parents' separation, establishing a career in the local entertainment scene as a model and actor. It was only in 2013, at twenty-five years old, when she decided to join Binibining Pilipinas, the country's largest beauty pageant, the winner of which gets to represent the Philippines in the Miss Universe competition. It took her three tries before Pia finally became that representative.

After being crowned Miss Universe, Pia became an instant international celebrity, representing global brands and organizations. She has become a staunch advocate of HIV/AIDS awareness and its eradication, as well as mental health and well-being.

Seven years after her reign as Miss Universe, Pia continues to find ways to inspire people all over the world. Aside from having a strong modeling career, Pia now leads a podcast aptly titled 'Between Us Queens' and, along with her co-hosts and fellow beauty queens, Carla Lizardo and Bianca Guidotti, spills exclusive pageant life stories and talks candidly about life as a woman.

Pia shares her wisdom on staying fit, managing relationships amid a pandemic, taking care of one's mental health—and what she wants to achieve further, as one of the most influential women of her generation.

On living one's best life and maintaining a relationship amid a pandemic

Before 2020, I had an idea of what was going to happen tomorrow, the next week, the next month—and work was the number one priority. But with everything that happened in the world in the past two years, it taught me how to slow down a little bit and to re-assess everything that I was doing, and to ask myself again: am I really happy with what I'm doing? Am I doing something meaningful with my time? Is this what really makes me happy?

I've been more focused on building a community to support women empowerment and, at the same time, taking care of myself, my health, and my well-being. It has been a challenge the past few years, but I feel like I'm going in the right direction.

With my relationship, specifically, I just had to be honest about the kind of work that I do and that it requires me to be in front of the camera all the time. It's really just having that open communication with each other—but also having plans. That's important in any relationship. You have to have something to look forward to.

On her identity crisis post-Miss Universe

When you watch Miss Universe from your own home, you turn on the TV, you watch the show, they pick a girl at the end, she gets crowned, the credits roll, and that's it. End of the show. But that's actually not the end. That crowning moment is the first day. That's the first day of the rest of your life, of the rest of your destiny. So, to me, I was very happy when I won because that was my big dream. But I was happy every day reporting to work. I was happy every day doing whatever that I needed to do, whatever that mission the organization asked me to do. It was my dream; I was very happy to be part of it. But after I passed on my crown, then I had to ask myself: what do I do now? Who am I without this? Who am I without the crown?

I had a mini identity crisis after because I prepared for so many years to get it, but nobody ever prepared me for the moment when you have to give up the crown. And that could go really bad if you don't take care of yourself and you're not surrounded with good people who won't take advantage of you and will give you good, sound advice. I was very lucky that I always somehow knew what the right thing to do was and which direction to go. I'm still following that. Even though it has been seven years now since Miss Universe, I'm still working on the advocacies that I genuinely find interesting, that I genuinely believe in. That's why I think that Miss Universe kind of opened the door for me. I wouldn't want to think of it as the peak or the highlight of my career. It was an instrumental and essential part for the rest of the things that I was going to do.

On the challenges of dating, as a successful woman

I did feel that guys were intimidated by me. They get intimidated when I don't talk, and they still get intimidated when I speak. It didn't really bother me a lot because then I just thought to myself: well, I just have to find the right guy. And I just have to find the right one who would be okay with me because what am I supposed to do? Am I supposed to water myself down for somebody else, so that I could be 'not intimidating'? It's not like I'm being like this on purpose. So, I understand how Miss Universe can be intimidating for a guy. Now I don't think that's the girl's fault, honestly. There has to be work coming from both ends. The girl has to obviously make the guy feel secure, reassure him; constant communication, open communication, honesty, and trust is so important. And, of course, the same with the guy—the guy has to let you have your moment.

On her podcast, 'Between Us Queens', and its growing community

The Queens community that we're trying to build is something that happened by accident. I have friends from *Binibining Pilipinas 2014*, two of my really good friends—and we all competed against each other—but we became really good friends and we always wanted to do a project together, but we weren't sure what it was going to be. At first, we thought, let's do a makeup vlog or that sort, but it didn't really push through.

So we did a podcast first about pageants for a year, and then we noticed that there were some months where there were no pageants. We noticed that whenever we sat down a beauty queen and spoke to her, we talk about pageants a little bit, but we talked more about her life, what she's doing now and you know the challenges that she went through and the conversation just feels more real and more relatable to people. And then slowly we started to shift to life, women's issues, social issues, and slowly began leaving pageants behind. So, then we said: why don't we start a podcast just talking about life in general? Everything—relationship, career, love, family, body issues—that a woman goes through.

Body issues is a most requested topic. It became timely also because it was at the start of the pandemic and people were becoming more inactive, because you're at home and there's not really a lot of space for you to move around. So, our bodies changed, and more women wanted to talk about that.

So, we get our cues from our audience. Because there's three of us who lead the podcasts and the workbooks and the discussions are also women, we have our personal stories and experiences to share aside from the community. It's really all very community-driven.

On weight loss and staying in shape

Weight loss is a big question; we get asked that all the time especially because I think we all came from pageants. We always get: 'Why is it so hard to lose weight?', 'What are your diet tips or diet secrets?', 'How do you stay skinny?', 'How do you look good in a swimsuit?'

We try to debunk these myths about dieting. We've been there; we've tried all the fad diets. We've tried the shortcuts, so we know what works and what doesn't work. We know that, yeah, you will lose the weight quickly, but you'll also gain it back much faster. You know we've made the mistakes and we're sharing our knowledge so then you guys don't make the same mistakes that we did before. And the good thing about us, having competed more than seven years ago now, is that we can be open about it. We can be honest; we don't have that filter any more. I'm just honest to the audience, and so are Karla and Bianca. And we also get advice from the community, because there may be some things that we missed out on, stories that are interesting, that are worth sharing.

One thing that I'm not going to do: I'm not going to starve myself any more. I used to do that—like, anorexic levels. I was so skinny before, and everybody was, like, wow, how do you do that? I just didn't eat. But then my mental health also suffered. I may have looked good in clothes, but then I couldn't think because I didn't have any nutrients in my body. You can't answer questions as sharply and as quickly as you used to. And you are not good at memorizing, you're always in a bad mood. There's really a tradeoff.

I'm also not going to do the fad diets, like taking only soup. I mean, I guess if you're detoxing and cleansing, it works for that. But if you're just trying to lose weight for a competition, it's not going to work.

Taking laxatives and diuretics are also a no-no. We've tried that already as beauty queens and it doesn't work; your body will suffer, your kidneys will suffer, your gut will suffer, your health will suffer.

Also, another thing: I remind myself not to be so hard on myself. A lot of times, I go back to an old picture from when I was competing and then I think okay, I looked good back then. But at that time, I felt like I wasn't enough. So, there's that negative talk then, negative thoughts in your head, that insecurity speaking also.

The best way is to educate yourself on the right kind of diet, and to keep yourself active. Weight loss shouldn't be the main goal. You won't be able to sustain it if your only purpose is to lose weight, because then it won't stick. It's not going to become a lifestyle. We're not after perfection, but progress.

I've learned that there's no magic pill to staying in shape. It's a slow and steady process, and it requires you to really invest in yourself—but it's not expensive. You just need a lot of water. You need to choose wisely what you're going to put inside your body. I'm not perfect at it. There are times where I have to remind myself all the time. I have a jug that can carry one liter of water, so I make sure to finish one to two jugs; if it's summer, three. Also, be active. When I say 'be active' or 'work out', people automatically think, I have to do a one-hour high intensity interval training (HIIT) workout. That's actually not true. A workout for me could not be the same level of intensity for somebody else. It's still counted as, you know, being active and moving your body. It doesn't mean you have to run a marathon. The thing with working out is, if you're starting from absolute zero, to have fun with it. Don't push yourself to a point where you wouldn't want to do it again tomorrow. I would rather have thirty minutes every day, then only do once a week or twice a week. You don't have to be at a gym to do it. You can do it from home. There're so many ways to do it at home now, through YouTube and through streaming. You can do it with your friends so there's accountability. Having a buddy makes it fun.

Even long walks really work, or just take the stairs. There're always those moments every day in our lives when we decide: am I going to take the shortcut or am I going to put in the work?

I am thirty-two now and I don't have any kids yet. My sister is thirty, and she has two kids. And just by observing her, I think: well, if I'm going to wait a few more years, I want to be at a fitness level where I can still run after them, that I can still chase them, that I can still carry them, and I won't hurt my back if I bend over and pick them up. The same for my everyday activities—I don't want to feel pain when I have to carry my suitcases, when I have to carry my bags, when I have to do the long hours of work that I have to do. In order for me to keep doing what I love to do, my body needs to be in good form.

On mental health

I appreciate that there is so much more awareness on mental health compared to five, ten years ago, especially in the Philippines. Before, when someone says they're depressed, the reaction would be, oh, they're just being dramatic. This wasn't too long ago, and I love the direction that we're now taking, our conversations—people are now becoming more aware. It just so happened that everyone was also affected by a pandemic that changed our lives. It tested our mental health, all of us. Each person has his or her own battles that they struggle with, and what is a problem for you may not be a problem for me.

Mental health, in general—I think we still have a lot to do in the Philippines. We still have a long way to go; we have less than 1,000 registered psychiatrists for the entire country. That's an alarming number. I think it's also because of the whole stigma around it, but I'm glad we're slowly starting to talk about it. It has encouraged me to share my experiences, too. I shared it during my TedxPH Singapore talk, and from time to time I also share it on social media. It's not something I would have shared years ago, because I didn't want to be seen as a Miss Universe who's weak, who's going through so many things, that I'm a fraud.

Initially, I didn't want help; I think a lot of people can relate to that. At first, you're hesitant, and you think, I don't need it, or I'm fine, I can handle this on my own. There's that denial. But then a person who cares about you and loves you will take notice and will probably do the first step for you. And then you'll realize that, okay, maybe I could benefit from this.

I went through a few sessions with my psychiatrist in New York and I remember thinking to myself, why did I never do this before? Like, I had to wait until I was twenty-six years old to talk about my childhood trauma, my struggles—and I had already won Miss Universe. So why is this manifesting itself now, at a time when I should be living my life because I just got my big dream? But that's how you know that fame or money doesn't buy happiness, and whatever issues that you are bearing inside that you are not facing will come back and will haunt you again in your adult life. It also made me think that there really shouldn't be a stigma around it.

If you are going through anything, anything at all, it should be normal to seek a professional. I started giving that advice to my other friends and family whom I felt like needed it also.

Fast Talk with John

What makes you Filipino?

What makes me Filipino is how much respect and importance I give to elders, to my family—how I put them first, how I put relationships and connections first, how I love to celebrate small wins. I find a reason to celebrate anything, and Filipinos are like that. We found a reason to come together. We also know how to smile and lift each other up, no matter how bad the times get. Filipino humour is amazing. It's unlike any other in the world.

For someone who has never been to the Philippines, is there anything from the Philippines that you would like for that person to see?

Something that I noticed is that no matter how beautiful a place is, the scenery, the beaches, if the people are not nice, it ruins the whole experience. If the people are not hospitable, nice, welcoming, warm, I wouldn't want to go back. So aside from what we have to offer—we have mountains, we have beaches—what I'm really proud of are the people.

If you were to give a commencement speech right now, what message would you give to a lot of the students who are coming out of school?

My advice would be not to rush things. A lot of things will happen. There will be ups and downs. There will be doors that will close on you. There will be moments when you will feel like you've hit a dead end. Or you will start to question your decisions, you'll start to question yourself, you'll start to question other people. But that's all part of the process. Don't try to resist it because that's where you get stressed. Just enjoy it and take in all the opportunities that you can. If there's a chance for you to do something one more time, try it again. If there's a chance for you to try something new, give it a go.

What gets you up in the morning? What helps you sleep at night?

What gets me up in the morning is really the motivation to go after my goals and to do the things that I really want to do. I always write stuff down; I really believe in the power of writing things down and then planning so then I know what's going to happen tomorrow. I know there's a plan, and I just have to show up and actually do it. So what keeps me going in the morning is knowing that I have something that's waiting for me. And at the same time, that's also what helps me sleep better: knowing that I didn't waste the day.

What is the one thing that you wish you knew sooner?

I wish we were taught about the right kind of way to take care of ourselves at an early age, because they don't really teach this in school or at home—like how to take care of your mental health, sexual orientation, gender identity and expression (SOGIE), taxes. I just feel like there are easier ways to educate teenagers so they would know how to navigate life easier. I mean, it's easier for the Now Generation because there're so many resources online; you can join so many communities and feel connected and get the knowledge that you need.

What will your epitaph say?

The kind of legacy that I want to leave behind is a story of somebody who was unafraid to share or to be open. I'm not embarrassed to share where I started and the challenges that I went through. I'm not embarrassed to share that we were really struggling when I was younger, and that I went through mental health problems. People see me as a Miss Universe, but I also want people to see the other side of the glitz and the glamour, the heels, the makeup, the crown. I want them to see real life. I want to be remembered as a beauty queen who is also a real person with real life experiences, and real struggles and real stories.

Is there anything specific that you do that you could share with us, that we could try to recommend, for our own selves, for our lives?

I think something that we could all try, and what's really helped me, is just writing your thoughts down. It really helps, even if you feel like you don't really need it. And I don't mean just writing a to-do list of the things you have to do today, but just writing your own thoughts. Some of us tried writing in our diaries, right, and didn't it feel like you were speaking to a friend? You're speaking to a safe space, like a person who would just keep your secrets, just as long as nobody reads your diary. Journaling can also feel the same way now that we're grown up. I always write a New Year's resolution, but I also write a mid-year's resolution, sort of like a check-in. Again, it's never about perfection. It's all about just progress, just keeping at it all the time.

My Thoughts

Like Pia, my therapist also recommended that I write my thoughts down in a journal. This is something that I felt I didn't need to do before, since I've always felt self-aware and in touch with my feelings and emotions. My therapist however pointed out the importance of keeping a record of my thoughts, having something to look back on that really examines my state of mind at a particular moment in time. Having this snapshot will enable me to realize perhaps at some point in the future of how far I've come. This will allow me to draw a mental map of who I am, who I'm not, and who I would like to become in the future.

Writing things down on paper is one of the most soul nourishing and even sensible activities one can do. From a business perspective, during times when I am trying to come up with new business ideas, I would purchase a large drawing pad so that I could fit into one page a kind of mind map of a business that I want to build. It would have different components of the business model, the partners I need to involve, the resources that I would need, etc. There's just something about starting with a clean, blank canvas and filling it with words and arrows of relationships of how something can work that creates a picture of what needs to be done to get something from nothing to something. From that one pager, I would be able to determine the next steps of who I need to talk to, what needs to be done, and in what order of importance. The end goal should be there as well.

From a personal perspective, my wife and I, a few years into our marriage, were introduced to an interesting writing exercise when we attended a Worldwide Marriage Encounter Weekend. It's a weekend retreat for married couples who want to further nurture their relationship, guided by other married couples and a priest. I don't want to get into the religion aspect but the activity of going through the weekend sharing, not to other people but to your spouse, feelings that maybe have not been communicated is a very helpful and nourishing activity to do together.

One of the best parts of the weekend is the writing of the love letters. You select a reflection topic or question to think about. The questions always ask you to talk about your feelings, which you should write down and eventually share with your spouse. The questions are wide-ranging and can be anything from something that recently happened, to your thoughts on a future idea or situation. You give each other five minutes to write (the time can also depend on you), after which you share and read each other's letters, and talk about your thoughts and feelings after.

Because many married couples do not know or need a little bit of help or guidance on how to communicate, writing your thoughts on paper gives you the opportunity to write focusing on your feelings, and eventually perhaps coming to some sort of resolution in the future. What's important is that you take the time to write things down, and eventually express them to your partner.

Sample questions would be:

1. How would I feel if we have another child?
2. When did I last compliment you? How does my answer make me feel?
3. How do I feel about our current financial situation?
4. How do I feel about growing old?
5. How does the 'busy-ness' of our lives affect our sexual relationship? How do I feel about that?

The answer should be in a love letter form—not in the sense of it being romantic or cheesy, but intentional to express your feelings and emotions. You can give yourselves five minutes or so to write, and at the end of the time allotment, you share your 'love letter' with your partner. The discussion is not meant to solve any problem, issue, or conflict right then and there, but just to hear the thoughts of your partner. It's not a time to blame or point fingers, but to express your feelings with the intention that your partner will know what you are going through or gaining deeper insights into your thoughts and emotions.

Chapter Assignments

You don't have to be Miss Universe to have the habits and virtues of one. What has made Pia truly exceptional is her life during and after her reign as queen, and her ability to face the pressures through mental honesty and fortitude. Try these hacks to help you with your mental and emotional game which can, in turn, nurture your soul:

- Get help. A psychotherapist can do wonders for your emotional well-being and can help you make sense of a lot of deep-seated emotions and issues you never even knew you had.
- Be honest with yourself. Whether it's setting a weight loss or fitness goal, maintaining a diet, or being in a relationship. Honesty is setting realistic expectations and goals that are achievable and something you can sustain for the long haul. Write things down if you have to. There's nothing like the power of your written word to serve as spiritual windshield wipers to aid you in putting clarity into your thoughts.
- Be part of or build a community. Whether it's a community of two or three people or two or three thousand. It always helps to have like-minded people who understand and support your needs and aspirations.

Brandon Vera

Mixed martial artist
ONE Championship heavyweight titleholder

**'Have I done enough? One more round. One more lap.
One more session. One more sit-up. It's part of the game
and I absolutely love it. And I'm scared to not have that.'**

Grind and make sure that sword stays sharp

Brandon 'The Truth' Vera is a fighter in more ways than one.

*He's known to most as a mixed martial artist and ONE Championship heavyweight
titleholder. But, he has been a fighter all his life.*

Born to an Italian mother and Filipino father, Brandon was raised by his Filipino stepmother in a Pinoy household in Norfolk, Virginia.

While he has mixed-race heritage, Brandon is proud of his Filipino roots. However, he grappled with backlash from those who criticized him for not being 'Pinoy enough'. But that doesn't stop him from representing the country and bringing honour to it.

Brandon is also no stranger to bullying, growing up as an overweight kid. He was even bullied into wrestling, and now he's thankful for the experience. He had successfully turned what looked like misfortune into one of his biggest achievements in life.

He was a collegiate wrestler, served in the United States Air Force, and joined the military's Greco-Roman wrestling team. In 1999, after being medically discharged due to an arm injury, Brandon began his extensive rehab and went on to study the art of submission grappling.

Soon, he trained in mixed martial arts under some of the best coaches in the world, and he's been a professional competitor since 2002. He has formally competed for the Ultimate Fighting Championship Mountain West Conference (UFC MWC) and later joined Singapore-based ONE Championship.

At ONE Championship, Brandon held the heavyweight world title for five years, becoming the longest reigning titlist in the promotion's history.

Today, apart from working to regain his belt, he plans to develop the next generation of Filipino martial artists at his very own Alliance Training Centre Philippines.

On getting into wrestling

Wrestling was definitely not something I wanted to be a part of, that I was looking to go try. In all honesty, I got bullied into wrestling. I was a fat kid who ate everything. My nickname in the family was 'Trash Compactor'. I would eat four Big Macs, with four french fries. And then, I would eat everybody's food at the table. Fat kid, super fat, spoiled American kid.

My cousin, Alan, was a bully at the time. He told me, 'You're fat. You need to come to wrestling. If you don't want me to beat you up every day, show up to practice.' I ended up joining the wrestling team. and I absolutely hated it. But Alan went to every practice, so I had to go to every practice.

Wrestling is a sport, you're either going to love or you're going to hate it. I hated it. But I had to grind it out because my hand was forced because of my bully cousin, who I am so very thankful for now. Because after my first year of wrestling, in the second year when I was in seventh grade, I fell in love with wrestling.

I started to learn; actually did a move that I watched on a tape, and it worked. It was crazy to me that I could actually do something, I could actually make something happen by myself with my own hands. Everybody wants to talk about the small leotards. I want to talk about the long hours of training, or the long distances and tournaments that last 48 hours, and how wrestlers always smell, and it's always wintertime. It's a hard sport. I'm okay with that. I enjoyed the grind.

Is wrestling for everybody? No, wrestling is definitely not for everybody. But I will tell you this, starting with wrestling, and then moving through my career, moving through life, and then moving through all the way up to now: any wrestler who is worth his or her salt, and competed at a high level or understood the wrestling game, and tried to get to the highest levels available at wrestling, all of them are super successful in life. Because once you're on that wrestling grind, everything else is easy. It's that wrestling grind is not fun, and you don't get paid for it. It's more just for pride. It literally is just for your pride. So, if you can do that, and with no money, yeah, everything else becomes very easy.

On his mixed heritage

My birth mother was Italian and mixed with a bunch of other things, American. My mom, the lady who raised me, she's Pinay from the Philippines. So, I grew up in a super Pinoy household, with *lola* staying on the couch. You know, like, we grew up Pinoy, no shoes in the house. The only thing we watched on TV that was American were cartoons. And I think *Days of our Lives*? Back in the day, some soap opera that lola would watch. We only spoke Tagalog at the house.

Everybody can say racism is not a thing, it's not real. Okay, let's say it's not real. Within the world, moving around the world, our African-American counterparts are always looked down upon for whatever reason. I'm talking about worldly views. Our Mexican counterparts in the world of Spanish or Hispanic people are looked down on. Us Filipinos as a whole, the southeast Asia area, we, as a people, are looked down on in the Asian world. And I think learning this as I grew up—I grew up in the South, I was a half-brown, half-white kid that grew up in the South, I wasn't white, I wasn't black—I had to find my own way. And I found out that people thought that Filipinos are the lowest class citizens of Asians. So, man, I had a long road to home. There's no rulebook, there's no handbook on how to figure this out.

The one thing that was steady in my life, like no matter what happened, my dad always went and opened the restaurant. My dad owned five or seven restaurants throughout his restaurateur career. Open, close, struggling, about to go broke, we're not eating this month, but everybody else is because he's the owner, he is paying everyone else before himself. No matter what, my dad got his ass up and went to work. Never ever, ever complained. My dad went through the wringer. He's been hacked on with a meat cleaver. He's been shot at, he's been robbed, he's been beaten on the head with a club. No matter what, my dad will go back to work. And he would say, you know, 'I'm just tired, *mahal. Pagod lang kaunti. Hayaan mo*, okay *lang*.' (I'm just tired, love. I'm just a little tired. Don't worry, it's okay.) And my Dad will always say this, 'Brandon, *hayaan mo. Kahit ano kayang-kaya ng Pilipino.*' (Brandon, don't worry. We Filipinos can do anything.) I was like, 'what?', and I didn't understand it, but he said it all the time growing up.

And now that I'm older, now that I'm wise to the world, I see how things move. I understand. Mother Nature can't kick our ass. People can't kick our ass, me losing our title from our last event doesn't sadden me as much. I'm going to come get that thing back. We just get over things. We make things happen.

Let's put this back the other way. Being a proud Pinoy and coming back to the Motherland trying to get my citizenship and trying to become a spokesperson for the Philippines. Man—I'm not Pinoy enough, I didn't grow up in the Philippines, I'm not brown enough. I was never poor enough. I don't know what it was like to be a real Pinoy. But 'racism is not real', right? You know, it's all of these things that we have to deal with throughout our lives and nobody ever talks about. Every day is a struggle, especially being a half-breed. That's part of what makes me who I am. That struggle and that grind, I welcome every day. I'm used to this game. This ain't my first rodeo. We've been doing this since I got bullied into wrestling.

On filming *Buybust* and being an actor

It's the same, but different. Two dances, one dance, both of you are trying to be the lead. That's in the circle of ONE Championship. On set, both of you're trying to figure out how to dance together, changing the lead, depending on the component of the set, what's needed for that scene. It's really, really cool. And how is it different? It's a lot easier when somebody is letting you lead them as opposed to trying to stop you from doing everything that you're trying to do. But I will say it's almost the same, in the respect that the output that I'm putting in is almost exactly the same. The intensity is the same, the cardio is the same, the struggle is the same. The only thing that I would take out of that is the anxiety of somebody really trying to kick you in the head and putting you to sleep.

I think even on set one time, I might have thrown up in between sets and I needed a second because I couldn't go again. It's demanding. Like action movies, I understand why action stars are the highest paid actors in the world. You have to remember lines, then spread around and do a thirty minute workout, and then repeat lines again. So, the hardest part for me about the movie was really not messing up. The movie set was full of the greatest actors that ever were. Everyone, anyone who's anyone is on that set. So, I didn't want to mess up because I was messing up for something stupid. I think that was the most anxiety I had. But other than that, it was so, so fun. God, it was fun.

I did a lot of line reading. I did a lot of roleplaying. I did a lot of acting workshops. And you know, the role was tailored exactly for what I could do for my first time on screen. But the load of work was the exact same as everyone else. They didn't take it easy on me. I had to do everything everyone else was doing. The action stuff. They had no problems with it, but we're doing lines and readings and details and expressions. Oh my god, talk about fish out of water. I was so new. I'm glad that everybody was so kind and so helpful. And teaching me along the way, because it's basically On-the-Job Training (OJT) for me, it was OJT and everyone was so helpful man. So, thank you, everybody.

On preparing for a fight

I start watching films of my opponent, I stalk them online. I follow them. I become immersed in everything that they're doing. I hope that they're posting training pics, I hope that they're showing techniques they're working on, because then I go to the gym, and I work on stuff and I go train. If I feel like this guy's already been to the gym, at least on Instagram (IG) or Facebook, I need to go back to the gym. It's a great motivating tool for me to use anxiety. And usually, you're training two times a day, sometimes three times a day.

If you're doing three days, one of those is technique. If you're training right, you're waxed, after you're done training you usually just sleep. The only time sleepless nights come is at the end of last training after the last nap. I'm running 1,000,000 times, scenarios in my head of what could happen. What else I need to train on what I should be training on? Have I done enough? Should I do more? One more round. One more lap. One more session. One more sit-up. It's part of the game and I absolutely love it. And I'm scared to not have that. I don't know what I would do with myself without it.

On peak performance and longevity

The way I train has changed. I don't spar hard. Every week, twice a week, for one fight, I might spar hard once or twice. The rest of the time, it's technique sparring, timing sparring. We're rolling really hard, we're wrestling live, we're doing everything else live. But the impact stuff, we've been staying away from. We sharpen the sword on our impact stuff now. Instead of sparring five rounds, I will do ten rounds of Holland drills, back and forth, all day long, over and over. That would be one of my training sessions.

When I slip punches and they're touching me but not really touching me, and I'm countering and leg kicking and I'm landing perfectly, it's because I'm doing these Holland drills. It's because my sword is sharp. I just need to be able to swing it the entire time. So, all we do is just grind and make sure that that sword stays super sharp. That's all we can do now. We stay away from the injuries; we rehab all the time. I probably go to physical therapy twice a week, massage two or three times a week, cryotherapy maybe during camp every other day. There's a huge learning curve for this. I didn't just get here. You know, it's been practice. It's been trial and error. It's been peaks and valleys. And it's been a lot of money. A lot of learning.

New age technology, cryo replaces old school ice tub soaking baths or cold baths. They use liquid nitrogen off into a super fine gas mist in a cylindrical standing form, so it shoots in the sides, neck down and brings your outside temperature down. They use a temp gun to check your skin and you're only in there for three minutes. Some places will let you raise your core temperature again and you jump back in for another three minutes.

After sparring, if I've done that three times my body is brand new. Instead of limping and gimping, I'm just walking around, no problems. It brings your temperature down so fast that the blood has to rush to the surface. I don't know all the scientific properties, but it works much better than an ice bath and it's three minutes as opposed to twenty.

On losing his title and working to regain it

I want my title back. That's the most important thing to me right now. It's not really the age. I don't think about that unless and until people ask me. For me, I just need my title back. I was off that night. Something was really off that evening. There is no age.

I don't know exactly what happened. I can't blame it on anything, except for myself. It's my fault. It could have been a series of events, but what it really boils down to is I did not perform the way that I trained, in the way I should have. And that's burning my ass more than anything else. Because no matter what happens to the world, my job is to go out there and kick Arjan's ass, and for whatever reason, that didn't happen. That's something I have to live with, that I have to eat and deal with, for the rest of my career. I'm just annoyed at myself.

I'm very much looking forward to rematching Arjan. I'm very much looking forward to getting our belt back. And, man, even to this day I still haven't watched that fight because it was so bad. While I was in the damn fight, in the circle, I remember thinking to myself, 'Yo, man, I fucking suck right now. What the hell are we doing? Move! Move your ass. What are you doing? Move bitch move!' I'm yelling at myself in my head and I'm so tired. I'm thinking about everything else. Like, I don't know what the hell was going on. And during my interview, people said, 'Brandon, your interview was crazy.' I remember thinking I've never been like this in my entire life, in my entire career. Like never ever. In all honesty, like I shit the bed, that's what it felt like, that's exactly what it looked like. But instead of just it happening, I was watching myself shit the bed while it was happening, you know? So, I had to deal with that for a little bit.

Fast Talk with John

What do you do apart from training and preparing for fights?

Still train once a day. Other than that, I hang out with my family, with baby Atreyu, my wife, and my brothers. In the Philippines, we had a gym set up in my backyard. We just trained and enjoyed family time.

What is it about you that makes you truly not just Asian but Filipino?

My attitude of *walang atrasan*. I don't know how to explain it more for anyone who hasn't been to the Philippines. I don't think I have the words to explain that other than the literal meaning of it means no retreat. If you want to get real cliché it's there would be no retreat, no surrender.

If you were to invite people to come to the Philippines, what is it about the country that you would like for them to discover?

I would show them Muntinlupa, Tondo. I would take them to all the towns and the *barrios* made out of bamboo that stick over the water. I will show them how those people live. I will show them how happy they are. I would show them how you can be happy with nothing.

Then, I will take them to all the five-star hotels that the Philippines has to offer. Then, we'll go find ourselves for maybe like three days in the jungle. And I would ask them, man, so what's important to you now? What have you seen that makes you think a little bit differently on this trip?

If I could tell people coming over to the Philippines, I want you to go out there and put some work in. Show people that you care. Don't do photo ops, don't IG post. Let's go to the farthest parts of the *bayans* that nobody knows about. Let's bring them some clothes, some stuff they've never seen before. Let's go and put some smile on people's faces that you would have never met sitting on your couch at home YouTubing all day.

Who are your heroes? It could be an athlete, it could be a CEO, it could be a politician, it could be anyone who to you is your modern-day superhero.

I have two sets. As I grow and experience life as the world turns, my number one heroes are my family, first generation. My uncle signed on the dotted line in the Navy, not thinking to do twenty years, just so he can sponsor his family to America. Now, he can get everybody to America. Now, these people from the Philippines, they don't speak any English. They don't have dollars. They got to take whatever with them and then go to this place that they know nothing about.

My second set of heroes, this is huge because you don't know about this until you know about this. I am a fan of moms and dads around the world. People who have families on lock, really good families are hard, bro. Like I understand to mix all those personalities with the kids and with the timing with this and with that, man. I salute all of you. Good job guys, you're all doing great. Keep raising amazing children for our future.

If you have ever been given a chance to give a commencement speech in school, what message would you impart to the generation now that is coming into this world with so much uncertainty?

Keep it simple. 'For me, to all of you graduating, I applaud you. You have done something that I can't do. I wouldn't do what I actually quit trying to do. I'm not a fan of school, I absolutely hate, detest school. I hate when people tell me to do things and I have to do things at a certain time. So, you guys are leaps and bounds ahead of me already. Truth be told, half of you, maybe more, aren't going to use those degrees that you guys walked across the stage for. That's how it is, it's the way of the world. You won't pay all that school debt back. So right now, you stand there looking at me confused. Things are going to start getting really real. I just want to put things in perspective for you. So, when you walk across the stage, you understand your plan needs to start now. Right when you get to the end of that stage with a diploma in your hand. Now, not two weeks, not on vacation, not when you're roaming the world. You better get to it now.

The other half of you will use your diploma in whatever aspect you get into. You might even use your diploma in something else that you had no idea you would fall in love with. I would say one to three per cent of you are going to become world champions. And those are the ones I'm looking forward to seeing. And when I say world champions, I'm not saying you got to become a mixed martial arts (MMA) fighter, some kind of pro athlete, you got to win, put all these gold rings, no, no. You're going to be the one to discover something. You're going to be the one that changed the world. You're going to be the one to create something new that the world has never seen before. You are the ones that I'm looking forward to watching grow. My name is Brandon "The Truth" Vera. Family, I'm out!' That would be my commencement speech.

In the end, what would your epitaph say?

Here's a man who learned along the way. He did as best as he could. And he helped as many people as he could. There's always going to be shoulda, coulda, wouldas. Make sure you live your life better than his and make sure you have less shoulda, coulda, wouldas in yours.

If there's one thing that you could suggest that personally I try, anything that you do, whether it's something that's related to the sport or mentality wise, what would you suggest that I try that can help me in my own life or in anything that I do? Any suggestions that you would like for people in general to try?

If available, you should be getting one massage a week. It will and can change your life if you find the right masseuse. Because she'll stretch you and just rebuild all the parts that hurt. You're working your body all the time, let somebody else fix you, let somebody work on you.

My Thoughts

If there's anything I could take away from my conversation with Brandon Vera, it's that, despite not being born in the Philippines, he is more Pinoy than most Filipinos I know.

So, what did I apply that Brandon does? Since pre-COVID, I would get massages perhaps once a week, and I know it definitely helps with recovery, particularly after a heavy workout. Since massages were not new to me, I decided to try cryotherapy instead.

I immediately set an appointment with a cryotherapy facility in my city. I made sure I went immediately after a hard workout the day before and the morning of. I had heard of the chamber that puts you in -110 degree Celsius. The one I went to had three separate chambers. The first one was -60 degrees, the next one was -100 degrees, and the final one was -110 degrees. The owner of the facility, Jesse Co, agreed to join me on my very first attempt. The goal was to be in the coldest chamber for a total of three and a half minutes. We stripped down to our swim trunks as you have to have as little clothing as possible. We were in our socks and slippers, and he handed me a pair of gloves and earmuffs to cover our extremities. The initial cold blast entering the first chamber was quite the thrill and, before you know it, ten seconds later, you are ushered into the next chamber. Another ten seconds, you are at the third and coldest chamber, and by this time your body has been in the cold for a while and is starting to get uncomfortable.

Jesse asked me to do some exercises and big arm movements, and squats. When Jesse said 'three minutes remaining', you get a sense that time is warped and slowed down, just because of the discomfort you feel that makes you think you've been in the chamber longer than you actually have. He did push-ups, which I followed, and as we were exercising, I realized that the surrounding air in the chamber was slowly fogging up from the moisture of the condensation of our breaths. Two minutes into our session, the chamber was almost completely enveloped in a fog of mist, and I noticed that ice crystals had already formed on our arm hair and our eyebrows. It was that cold! The last thirty seconds were an incredibly tense countdown with every cell in my body wanting to just leave the chamber. 'Time!' Jesse finally says as he opens the door back to the second chamber where we stayed for a few seconds, and next to the first chamber before finally exiting.

As you step outside, you feel an overwhelming sense of euphoria and an endorphin kick unlike anything I've felt before came over me. This process of subjecting your outer skin to extreme cold is apparently the hallmark of a new science of sports. Having tried an ice bath before, I can say that cryotherapy is definitely a less painful, faster option.

I surmise that this won't be the last time I will try something new to try to maintain peak performance. Though I am not a professional athlete like

Brandon, I still aspire to maintain my health and athleticism in the coming years and even decades, making sure that the sword stays sharp.

Sidebar: Longevity Escape Velocity

I am acutely aware that I am not getting any younger, making me think of ways to try to see how I can extend my strong, productive years. This has also made me curious to try to find ways to maintain peak performance, and to explore the concept of age reversal.

The audacious idea that ageing is a disease that can be cured is one that was first put forth to me when I met Dr Peter Diamandis when I took the executive programme at Singularity University of which he is the executive founder.

Peter Diamandis believes we are nearing Longevity Escape Velocity or LEV (originally coined by biogerontologist Aubrey de Grey in a 2004 paper), where science and medicine can extend your life for more than a year for every year you are alive.

Think about it: for a majority of human history people had a life expectancy of twenty-five years, before the standard of living and enhancements to human well-being drove up life expectancy to what it is today. In the future, proponents of LEV believe a combination of factors such as precision medicine, biotechnology, regenerative medicine, gene therapy, nanotechnology, biometric monitoring, advanced prosthetics and virtual reality (as will be discussed by Chien Han How in a succeeding chapter), AI-enabled drug discovery, and many others, will essentially allow us to extend our lives to unimaginable lengths.

People like Peter, and colleagues such as futurist technologist Ray Kurzweil, believe we could reach this in our lifetime.

Though I have no immediate wish or intention to live forever, I do want to increase my health span, or the period of life spent in good health, free from chronic diseases and disabilities of ageing. This is something worth studying and exploring in the future.

Chapter Assignments

If you're a mature athlete like Brandon, you too can perform with the finesse and complexity of fine wine. On top of that, you can make your fellow men proud by staying true to your roots and making priceless contributions. Here are a few things you may want to consider:

- Train for your age. You may not be as fast or as strong, but you are definitely wiser and smarter than your younger self. Get science to help you out. Sauna, cryotherapy, hyperbaric chambers are some things you can consider trying out.
- Help uplift lives. Maybe you can donate your time or money to charities, join outreach activities, and pack relief goods. Be a volunteer teacher or devote your time to an animal shelter. This is the essence of who Brandon is, which he translates inside the ring.
- Watch *Buybust*. The 2018 film depicted one of the harshest realities in the Philippines at that time. Come for the gritty suspense and the thrilling action stunts, stay for the sobering finale. And note that this is Brandon's first acting gig, so be very, very forgiving.

Toby Claudio

Entrepreneur, athlete
President of Quorum International Inc., Toby's Sports,
Runnr, Urban Athletics

**'Focus, hard work, determination, discipline, teamwork
are just some of the things that sports teaches.'**

The business of sports and well-being

His father named the business after his son, and the rest is history.

Toby Claudio worked for another company after college, but he had always known he was going to one day work at the company named after him.

The business, which began as a toy store, eventually grew to become the sporting goods chain, Toby's Sports.

Now president of Toby's Sports, he later ventured into other sports-related businesses, including running the specialty store, Runnr and the street lifestyle retail store Urban Athletics.

Apart from being a sportsman and entrepreneur, he has developed projects that helped uplift the lives of many Filipinos as former president of the Manila chapter of Junior Chamber International (JCI).

On 'Toby's' and handling the family business

My case is very unique. I'd be lying if I said that I didn't know I would end up with a family business, because they put my name on the sign. That gave me no choice and kind of helped me decide what I wanted to do with my life. Like I always say, my name was my destiny; it was carved in plastic or panaflex or whatever. As soon as they put my name on the sign, I knew from an early age that this is something I want to do. Every day after school, I would walk from La Salle Green Hills to Greenhills and hang out in the store and wait for my dad to finish work. I saw firsthand how we grew from very humble beginnings, how we served our first customers, how we did it with such personal touch. My dad would literally measure hands to get people the right size and grip for their tennis racket, and my uncle and my dad were stringing rackets themselves. That really set a great foundation growing up around the business. It really helped me value all the work that they put into it and the legacy that they were passing on to me. They didn't force me to join the business right away; in fact, they were like, go ahead do something else first. I also wanted to see what I could do in the professional world.

I went into marketing brand management because it kind of gave me a good all-around view of business—not just marketing but everything; operations, sales, logistics. I spent two years with a different company, a bigger company. In those two years I was just soaking it up, learning from my bosses as much as I could. And then after two years, I realized I really want to contribute to the business now. I think that's invaluable. In fact, it's in our family constitution now that anyone who wants to join the business, say, for instance, my sons, they have to work a minimum of three years and if they want to come into the company at a certain level, they have to reach that level outside first.

On how Runnr was born

There were two things in my bucket list: one was to become the president of JCI Manila, another one was to start a new business. For some reason, that

had been on my list for more than five years and I've never moved; there was
no progress made at all on both of them until I started getting things done. I
simply put it down as a project: start a new business. The discipline is, okay, if
that's something you want to happen someday, what's the first step? My first
step was research ideas for new businesses and literally that's what I typed on
Google: ideas for new businesses. This is how clueless I was. I think the first
hit was a website selling logos for new businesses that had been designed by
artists but were rejected by those who commissioned those.

One logo caught my eye, just really stood out. It was called Runnr, R-U-
N-N-R, and the logo of a running man. The minute I saw it, I said, 'Wow, this
is a cool brand, and the logo, it's all set,' and it was I think for sale for around
$400. I said, 'Okay, it's nice but I don't need it, what am I going to do with it?'
I'm looking for a new business and, at the time, we only had Toby's. The story
is my father named it after me when I was five years old because it started out
as a toy store, and I was five so he said I'm not going to name it after myself.
His name is Bobby and he named it after his five-year-old kid, Toby. It was a
tiny hole in the wall in Virra Mall in Greenhills; he was probably too ashamed
to name it after himself. That's before it turned into a sports store.

But the significance of that was that I was always the son of the owner.
I did not start the store that bears my name, so that was always a chip on my
shoulder; that this is not by me, I didn't start this. I always wanted to start
something by myself so, long story short, a week later, I came back to the site
and this logo was still for sale and I just put in an offer of I think $100—one-
fourth of the asking price. I got an email back and it said, 'Thank you, I never
thought anybody would buy any logo of mine, I'm only a fourteen-year-old
boy from Indonesia.' I thought I was going to get a good deal; apparently, I
gave him the biggest paycheque. Sorry, now I remember it was $200, I didn't
lowball him that much. He got $200 from me but I didn't get just a logo. I got
the seeds, the inception for a new business.

I said, 'Wow, now I have to do something with this because I bought it; I
wasted 200 bucks if I don't use this.' That was 2008. In 2008, Bonifacio Global
City (BGC) was flat, there was nothing there. Because BGC was so open, so
empty but had all the streets, fun runs started happening every weekend. I
saw hundreds, eventually thousands of runners pass by my window. It was
not rocket science to think that hey, there might be an opportunity to finally
open up a running specialty store. But our sales in the running category at
Toby's at the time were minuscule, less than five per cent. It wasn't really a
thing back then. But I wasted $200 on a logo, and it was perfect for a store

and, following the getting things done protocol, I was forced to review all my projects to make sure that there's a next step. The next step was to come up with a deck to pitch a business plan for a running store. But before that step, I inserted another one and made an appointment with Ayala Corp., who owned Bonifacio High Street to present a deck. Had I not set the appointment, I don't know if I would have done the deck. I had two weeks to come up with a deck, so I did a lot of research online and came up with a concept for a world-class running specialty store, something that I think I would hope would hold its own against the best running specialty stores anywhere in the world. I knew exactly which space I wanted to get on Bonifacio High Street, and that's what I went to Ayala to pitch. They gave me the exact space that I wanted. They said, 'Perfect timing, the tenant there who's occupying the space was not doing so well so we're probably not going to renew his contract.' And because the CEO of Ayala is a triathlete, Fernando Zobel, they were all giddy and said, 'Oh Fernando would love this.'

The next six months were spent following the other steps; putting together the actual business, traveling to a few countries to conduct research, getting the brands that I wanted to feature in the store. I think about eight months after I bought the logo from that boy, we opened the store. True enough, Fernando Zobel helped us cut the ribbon. It was such a nervous moment for me because I had never put up a store other than Toby's; never a new business, never in a new category that was untested, unproven. I had no idea how this was going to happen, whether it would succeed but, lo and behold, on the first day, we had a line of people in front waiting to come into the store. But the best reward for me was when Fernando came in, checked out the store, walked through the store, and then he came up to me and said, 'Whenever I'm in a foreign country, I make it a point to visit the best running store in that city.' He said, 'This is the best running store I've ever seen.' I think, as entrepreneurs, that's what we live for.

In its first year, Runnr set so many records for us. It had the fastest return on investment of anything we've ever done, any store we've ever opened. It won the most promising retailer of Ayala Malls in its first year, it landed on the cover of Philippine Daily Inquirer as one of the top ten trends of 2009. We were the only store, the only brand on that list. It wasn't running as a trend, it was a Runnr as one of the top ten trends for the year. The next year, it won store of the year of Ayala Malls, which is something that even Toby's had not won till then. Now, we're up to four stores because we like to keep the network small. This year, we're finally launching our website, runnr.com.ph.

On giving people something they don't know they want

We definitely didn't go and ask people what they wanted. One quote that really struck me was Steve Jobs saying we should give people something they don't know they want. That's really what I was after. I wanted to create something that people have not seen in the Philippines yet. There was nothing happening in the running space yet; I just tried to figure out what that would look like and, from my own personal experience, it was really straightforward. I was running in the wrong shoes the whole time. I had been running in shoes which looked good, highly cushioned, but apparently, they were way too narrow and there was no support whatsoever for the midfoot area, for my arch, which is very low. I over pronate and apparently that's what causes stress on my knees and especially my back. I've had two screws in my knee, and I've had a history of slip discs. So running was not fun for me when I started out.

I wanted to get into those fun runs, but I couldn't even run from the house to the next corner before feeling some kind of pain either in my knees or my back. I had to study for myself what I was doing wrong and, apparently, I had the wrong running form. I had a very weak core and my lower Achilles, my calf, and my core were just way too weak to run, which led to my injuries. Lastly, I was wearing the wrong kind of shoes. I didn't even know, and I figured that's something that's worth providing as a service to consumers; being able to analyse them, figure out their gait and their foot type, and being able to prescribe footwear that's best for their foot type that will provide a little correction. And sometimes, for people who don't need correction or minimal shoes, that's really the product for me: selling a new lifestyle, getting people to try out running and then adopting it as their way of life.

We have products under our three brands—Toby's Sports, Runnr, and Urban Athletics—and around fifteen others, which we created ourselves, which we don't really shout out as local brands and people often mistake them for imported brands. The whole point was to offer the best value for money we could by branding it ourselves but sourcing good quality products from good manufacturers all over Asia. Unfortunately, we don't have much of the manufacturing here in the Philippines, so that's something that hopefully we end up being able to do down the road. But also, to create a brand made in the Philippines that is sold worldwide and respected as a global brand would be a great dream to accomplish.

On getting things done

When asked what books I would recommend to anyone if they want to become successful at anything, it's *Getting Things Done, The Power Of Habit* and *Spark: The Revolutionary New Science of Exercise and the Brain.*

Going back to getting things done, that book has a very simple formula. The best analogy is if you want to hit a good forehand in tennis, if you want to clear the pole vault, there's the right form, there's a way to do it that's been proven over time. The technique has been studied and perfected and it's just something that you have to learn and ingrain in yourself. When you can execute it without thinking about it, then you can successfully pull off that masterful stroke. Getting things done is simply the business equivalent of that. If you want to get something done, there's a formula to how you get from point A to point Z, and the book just gives you the step by step. What I love about it is it really opened my mind that the science behind being a master at sports can also be applied to work. It just made perfect sense to me because ever since I was a kid, I was watching replays of Andre Agassi's forehand, Roger Federer's backhand, among others, but when it comes to work nobody really tells you that there's a right and wrong way to do it. They just tell you to get on with it.

But now, after I studied and adopted the GTD system, the getting things done system, it's indispensable for me. I have it on my laptop and on my iPhone and even when something comes to me, whether it's a mundane task or a big project or just an errand, I jot it down on my phone and it automatically syncs to my laptop. You just have to break it down into really small tasks that are achievable, and the software organizes it for you and when you sit down and get to work, you just check off one by one those routine tasks. Ever since I adopted that, I've got a lot more work done; I have to say I am a lot more organized than I was. Before, I had the tendency to have so many things going on in my head at the same time, so I needed the system to really help me. It's one of the best habits I picked up, to be honest, late in life.

On how sports can change your life

I love sports and I saw how it helped me. By playing team sports, it taught me so many values that I consider to be indispensable in life. Focus, hard work, determination, discipline, teamwork are just some of the things that I think sports teaches. I think it's been helpful for me all the way through my career to my adult life. I really honestly believe that every kid growing up should have a chance to play sports so that they can learn all these values.

Try training for an Ironman triathlon and see how that changes you. I've been an athlete my whole life, but I could never really say that exercise changed me. It was something I liked to do, it was fun, I was part of the team and I enjoyed it, I competed. But when I trained for triathlon, that was the only time that I really experienced how exercise can change you. That's because of the volume of cardio training that I did. I would do 12–13 hours a week; that's about two hours a day for six days, sometimes twice a day, of running, swimming, or biking. That much cardio has effects, really changes you. I think my weight dropped by about 10, 15 pounds. I didn't even realize that I was fat back then, my body fat was I think around twenty plus and my cardio was really bad. I couldn't run, I had no endurance whatsoever.

But when I started training for triathlon, the changes to my body and my mind were significant. I noticed after a while that, on a day that I trained, in the morning I worked faster, I made decisions faster, I solved problems better, and I powered through the day. On days that I didn't train in the morning, I felt sluggish, indecisive, anxious, stressed, and ever since any time I would feel that I needed a boost, I needed to work on something difficult, solve a hard problem, or I was being brought down by anxiety, or I was worried about something, I put in an hour of vigorous cardio and the world is a better place.

On building a 'field of dreams' for poor children

Our chapter JCI Manila has been around for almost seventy years already. It used to be called the Jaycees. It's one of the leading leadership development organizations, not just in the Philippines, not just in Asia but also in the world. There are thousands of JCI chapters globally. JCI Manila has a long and proud heritage of developing young leaders below the age of forty.

It started with a very simple outreach. We went to an underprivileged, impoverished community, which lived right beside the biggest garbage dump in Metro Manila, which had been decommissioned many years ago. They called it Smokey Mountain because it's perpetually smoking because of, I think, methane or people burning trash. There's a community that has built their homes around it. The head of the community pulled me aside and said, 'Hey we do have a baseball field here.' I said, 'Okay, this I've got to see for myself.' Having been a baseball player since I was a kid all the way up to college in the University of the Philippines (UP), baseball is very close to my heart. I pulled together the rest of my board mates and we hopped over to the site. True enough, right in the midst of all the trash, they had cleared out a little open space which was overgrown with some grass but mostly dirt and garbage. They had set up a diamond and they were playing baseball there. They weren't even using gloves. They showed us the equipment they were using; they had fashioned makeshift baseball gloves from rubber sandals and cardboard.

But as I watched them throw and play catch, it actually made them really good baseball players, because to be able to catch a ball with just a piece of cardboard, you have to have very good technique. I think because we grew up in the eighties, we remember the Kevin Costner movie *Field of Dreams*. My directors and I looked at each other and said, we've got to turn this into a real, proper baseball field.

That year, 2010, my board and I came up with that project, Field of Dreams, as part of a bigger community development programme for Smokey Mountain called Dare to Care, because truly that community was so deserving of help. They live beside the garbage dump and earn a living scavenging and it's the whole family who scavenges—not just the adults, the parents, but even the kids. So, their parents don't encourage them to go to school. When we converted it into a baseball field, one of the best-looking baseball fields I've ever seen and played on in the Philippines, proper grass, proper landscaping, a backstop, all the kids just wanted to play.

There were thousands of kids in that community. But they made one brilliant rule: you couldn't play as part of the Smokey Mountain baseball or softball team if you didn't go to school and keep good grades. The best reward from that was seeing, to this date, I think, there have been more than ten kids who grew up in Smokey Mountain playing who have already earned scholarships to colleges in the Philippines. College scholarships to play softball and baseball, both boys and girls. Some have actually already graduated. That is one really good example of making a difference, starting from something small. By them graduating you're sure that their family has a different future ahead of them. It's a great case study really of how sports changes lives. Even from the onset the fact that the kids had a place to play, whereas before that area was where you would see a lot of kids using drugs because it was dark and secluded. From being on drugs to playing sports and joining tournaments, they even went abroad.

Fast Talk with John

What makes you Filipino or what makes you Asian? What sets you apart from the competitors that you saw when you were doing your research abroad?

I also grew up in the US, but I don't consider myself brought up the American way. I was there as a kid and what that helped me realize was how different we are. In many ways, I think Filipinos are not seen the right way. We are seen as fun-loving, very adaptable, but I think what not everyone sees is how competent and creative Pinoys really are. Even abroad, people are always a bit surprised why we speak English so well, we express ourselves so well, and we're capable of doing a lot of things, creating brands, creating businesses, developing stuff. We create stuff, we outsource so much of the work of so many other countries, so I think talent and creativity and competence are something that us Filipinos can be proud of.

What is the one thing that you feel Filipinos can share with the rest of the world? What is it that is uniquely us that you're proud of and you want people to know?

Definitely I think of our warmth. We're really friendly as a people, we're known for our hospitality. Anyone who's never been to the Philippines, I would strongly recommend you come and experience it firsthand. Foreigners who I run into abroad who have been to the Philippines all say the same thing, they had so much fun in Manila, in the Philippines, and the people are great. That's why we're also respected and so many countries recruit service personnel from us. Our retail personnel are all over the world because they're among the best salespeople.

I'd like to know if you have any heroes, whether it's an athlete, an entrepreneur, or a businessman. Who do you look up to and what qualities are present in that person that makes you look up to him/her?

It's ironic, they're two people who are totally different and I respect them for totally different reasons, and they were competitors their whole life: Steve Jobs and Bill Gates. Steve Jobs I really looked up to because, as an entrepreneur, I think he set a very high benchmark for what skill set an entrepreneur should have. He had vision and he was capable of inspiring people with that vision. It was very clear what he wanted to accomplish, and he was single-minded in that purpose. That's why he got it done—because he knew exactly what he wanted to accomplish. On the other side of the coin, Bill Gates was the same; he was brilliant but in different ways. He was technically brilliant but what really strikes me about him is after he had reached the pinnacle and did everything he could do to build his company, he moved on to the next stage of his life, which was to change the world and give back to society. He's single-minded in that focus now.

How I wish I could create something as big as the way Steve Jobs did it and then give it away the way Bill Gates is doing it. Those two really stand out for me because they lived with passion and purpose, they got it done, and it changed all our lives. With Steve, the products that he made, it changed the way people work, changed the way we used gadgets, and I think inspired people to be more creative as well. Then what Bill Gates is doing now is so inspirational because of the way he's trying to build something as big as he built it and now diverting his energy, his talent, and even his treasure to solving the most difficult problems that mankind is facing.

Have you ever given a commencement speech back in school? If you haven't, what would be the main message that you will give to the student body?

I have given a talk to high school students in Camarines Sur, but not a commencement speech. That's something that would be big for me because: one, I don't think I deserve it, two, I've always been asked to give talks before and I always start that by saying that you should never waste an opportunity to inspire people, so if you have that many people in a room at one time, I would definitely take that very seriously. What would I tell them? I think what's hard now is I'm sure people are scared that the future looks challenging. You really have to figure out what you want to contribute because that will dictate what you have to be good at, what you start, what kind of company your business you go into. There has to be a belief that, through my work I am contributing something of real value to others.

When you have a purpose behind what you're doing, no matter how hard it is or no matter how little enjoyment you get from it, you'll still keep at it. You won't give up on it because you truly and honestly believe that what you do makes a difference. That's my first piece of advice to kids; to figure out what you want to really contribute and why you want to do it. That will dictate what and how well you can stick to it because sticking to it, grit, getting things done all stem from having a purpose. Having a mission will keep you on the path and eventually lead to your success hopefully.

The other thing is I would recommend the three books: *Getting Things Done*, so you have a dream, what's the first step? You have to break it down into the easiest possible steps that will get you closer to where you want to go. If you just keep dreaming that, hey I want to be something big later on, but never have the discipline to break it down into small actionable steps, you're never going to get going. Getting things done as a skill should be taught in schools. Also read *The Power of Habit*. If you want to achieve things, you have to pick up the right habits. It's the habits you collect along the way which will scientifically determine the chances of you achieving what you want to accomplish. The last one is *Spark* because, as the book proved, our bodies were made to move and if you don't use it the way it was intended, you're never going to be an optimal human being, you're never going to perform at your best, physically, mentally, and even emotionally.

If there's anything that I could try right now, what would be your advice? Anything that I can take up that's going to be easy, something that I can maybe start tomorrow?

I believe in cardio so much so I would suggest you get a Bluetooth-enabled treadmill, and you just subscribe to an app and run on your treadmill, join events, run with a bunch of people. It's gamified, you won't get lazy doing it because there are incentives for you to hit certain objectives, goals, mileage, and it's just fun to do it with friends. Sometimes you work out, you do it by yourself, and there's no virtual aspect to it, it gets boring after a while. It's really a game changer when you do it with other people virtually, when you have a gamified experience along with the workout. It's a whole new world, really, for exercise.

My Thoughts

Since interviewing Toby on the podcast, which was done during the height of the pandemic when people were in lockdown in Manila, the world has opened up. At a time when Toby was doing the virtual route, I decided to get into cycling myself. For the first year, I got myself a road bike, and eventually after experiencing the roads for myself, I realized that gravel biking is most ideal for the road conditions and for the kind of biking that I want to do.

Think of a gravel bike as in-between a mountain bike and a road bike. The form factor is closer to a typical road bike with drop bars (as opposed to mountain bike bars that are straight), with wheel widths that are in-between thin road bike wheels and the thick mountain bike wheels. What this gives you is the ability to switch from main roads to literally off the beaten paths—the kind where adventure begins, and the unknown makes for an exciting proposition.

The joys of biking—whether with friends or alone—present their own distinct charm. With friends, you are after the camaraderie of not just the ride but of finding nice little pit stops where you get to have coffee, breakfast, or lunch together. Depending on your competitiveness, you also find that going in groups forces everyone to improve their relative time and speed, something that you will find is a natural progression for a group that wants to pursue improvements in general progression and fitness levels. I recently joined a gravel race where my buddy Mark and I were crossing rivers and pushing our bikes up impossibly steep inclines.

A solo ride is totally different, allowing you to be one with your thoughts and one with the road and your own body. Riding in a group is fun and makes for great bonding, while riding solo is good for the spirit and gives you time to be one with your thoughts. I've done a number of solo gravel rides where I just take random lefts and rights from a main countryside road, and find myself either in gravel or dirt roads, even volcanic ash at one point. It's just you, your bike, and your camera phone on a journey where you take everything in and take a few snapshots to remember your trip by.

Sports in general really has the ability to provide you with tremendous benefits beyond the physical. From allowing you the opportunity to write a new narrative for your future, as we have seen with the Smokey Mountain baseball kids, to giving yourself the chance to strengthen bonds with others and to be one with yourself and with nature.

Chapter Assignments

Toby is a firm believer that sports is beneficial not just for one's physical, but also mental and overall well-being. When training, you essentially improve so many aspects of your life in the process. If it gives you the opportunity to self-actualize yourself through sports, it can be your ticket to an improved version of you, and a better life. Try to take your first step with these options:

- Just run. Or swim. Or walk. Start with five or ten minutes and work your way from there. The breeze blowing on your face, the cardio workout, the endurance required—with hard work, these will all manifest not only in a sound body but also a clear mind.
- If you can, take it a notch higher by joining a race or a club. It could be your first 5K or the tennis club nearby offering a beginner's course. Exercising is one thing. Training for and actually competing in a race or tournament is a totally different and much more rewarding, well, exercise.
- Read the following books to get that dose of inspiration: *Getting Things Done*, *The Power Of Habit* and *Spark: The Revolutionary New Science of Exercise and the Brain*. Throw in *Shoe Dog* by Phil Knight and you've got yourself a handful that will not just inspire you but take your body and mind to new heights.

Ernest John 'EJ' Obiena

Olympian and all-time best Asian pole vaulter in history

'I live a life with no regrets.'

Breaking records

Filipino Olympian Ernest John 'EJ' Obiena has put the Philippines on the map of pole vaulting. After breaking records after records, he became the first Filipino athlete to qualify for the 2020 Tokyo Olympics. At the 2022 Southeast Asian Games, Obiena was the flag bearer and eventually won Gold. Obiena is no stranger to challenges. In college, he was intimidated by the rival university, which cost him a podium finish. In his professional career, controversies hounded him even if he practically carried the country's colours on his shoulders.

But for every hurdle he conquered, he only kept getting better and better. The promise Obiena shows in every meet brings hope not only to the future of the sport in the country but also to aspiring athletes who may be at the crossroads of their careers.

In this one-on-one—and heart-to-heart—talk with me, a fellow pole vaulter, Obiena opened up about his 'demons' and the desire to be the best pole vaulter in the world. This interview is the verbatim conversation between EJ and I on the podcast Methods to Greatness.

On his beginnings as a pole vaulter

JA: I've been waiting to do it for so long because like you, and I guess I can count on my two hands the number of pole vaulters that I personally know, I used to be a pole vaulter and I am very happy that someone like you has risen to prominence in such an obscure event. You are the best right now in Asia, one of the best in the world. And EJ I know that I will geek out. This is probably the most thrilled I've ever been to interview someone because of the fact that you are doing something that I've always wanted to do. And congratulations on all the success you've had through the years.

EJ: Thank you. Thank you very much. As you said, there are not a lot of pole vaulters out there in the Philippines and hopefully, we get to change that a little bit.

JA: I used to train with your father, Emerson Obiena, back in the 1990s. He was the men's champion and I was the junior champion. I remember those days very vividly. Very early days of pole vaulting in the Philippines. Can you give me any recollections that you have from when you started because I think when you started, I was already out of the sport. I'd like to find out how your father introduced you to pole vaulting.

EJ: The first thing I remember was not vaulting with the actual pole. I was vaulting the thing you used to raise the bar. That's the thing that I used because they're short enough for me and they're aluminum. We trained at Rizal Memorial Coliseum and the pole was on the starting line of the 100 metres. There was the old track, and that's my earliest memory when maybe I was like six years old. I was trying to clear those. There wasn't even a bar. It was just like a pit or a foam that my dad just put over the mattress where we landed. That was how it was. It was just fun games, and it was my ticket for a Happy Meal from the fast-food chain across the street. Track and field or specifically pole vaulting was my way to get the Happy Meal.

JA: For me, pole vaulting was a way to excel at something that not a lot of people really knew how to do as opposed to, say, something as common as the 100 metres. But for pole vaulting, it's different. It's something that not everyone can even attempt to do because of all the preparation that has to go into it.

As a kid who was just playing, you realized at some point that this is something you would like to take seriously because there are a lot more things at stake rather than just that Happy Meal down the road. What was the turning point for you just thinking that okay, now I am no longer just a kid maybe, this is no longer just a game?

EJ: It was slow progress towards realizing that what I'm doing is something serious; that it's something that I could be good at. When I got into high school, I wanted to win a lot of tournaments. But at that time, what does it matter? It's a competition. It's fun. But of course, I'm competitive. I learned at a very young age that I wanted to win.

In the last two years of high school, I wanted to get into a good school. We weren't in a position to send me to wherever I would want to be going. The best schools cost a lot. Luckily, athletics has the UAAP and National Collegiate Athletic Association (NCAA). I thought if I'm one of the best, I would be recruited. That's where I started to see that this is my ticket to a better future. This is something that would land me in the Big Four universities like Ateneo, University of Santo Tomas (UST), UP, and La Salle. I focused a little bit more on training and then when I reached university, I became part of the student-athletes programme where you need to study, and you need to perform. I eventually got to Ateneo.

On joining his first competitions

JA: What happened when you started to compete for Ateneo?

EJ: The first competition I competed for in Ateneo was the University Games in Bacolod. It was also the first time I was booed, and it was the first time I heard chants against me. I was hearing rival school 'Animo La Salle' every time I jumped. Every time I was jumping, I just felt so small. My hands were sweating. My coach then told me that it's okay to lose but not against La Salle. I lost. I wasn't able to perform. A few months after, it was UAAP. That time, I was thinking I just needed to zone in and just kill it. I won the meet at 4.30 metres. The guy from La Salle, I remember clearly, missed two attempts. Vindication! I said to my coach, 'I hope it was worth it getting me as your pole vaulter and not the other kids in my batch.' That was a different pride and sense of victory. It was beautiful.

JA: You only had your growth spurt when you were in college. Maybe early high school—I mean I think the physicality of being an all-around athlete needs to be there for you to be able to do well in the pole vault. You weren't physically mature at that time so what was that like for you? Were you successful as a pole vaulter in high school?

EJ: It would depend on how you define 'successful'. I was successful in getting a scholarship to the school that I would want to get into. Fun fact, I haven't won *Palarong Pambansa*.[7] My best record was silver. That's it. I never won. As a high schooler, I wasn't crazy good. You probably have more accolades in high school. I didn't have a record in high school. It was a tough journey.

JA: You remind me so much of Michael Jordan, who initially did not even make it to his high school team, but eventually became arguably the best basketball player in history. When I was in high school, you and I were the other way around. I was a little bit taller than most track and field athletes. When I was a sophomore, that's when I first held the pole and when I was a junior, that's when I broke the record in the UAAP for juniors in the pole vault. I won the gold in the Palarong Pambansa. So, it's actually mind-boggling to me that I'm talking to you now. You've never won gold but here you are now, an Olympian and the best pole vaulter ever in Asia. It just goes to show that early success or early failure does not necessarily translate to success or failure later on in your athletic career.

On the difference of pole vault training versus other sports

JA: What was it like training for the pole vault for those who do not know or are not familiar with the sport? If you could describe to me, first, the kind of training that you have to do to even be able to do this very complicated event. What were the skills that you had to learn?

EJ: The thing about pole vault is it's just so out of place for even track and field, which is like a lot of complicated movements. I think pole vault can be divided into three different parts: track would be the running part. Strength would be at that takeoff area, that is strength for me. Then gymnastics after that. If you divide that, you need to train like a track athlete, and you need to

---

[7] *Palarong Pambansa* or National Games is a national meet where the best high school and collegiate athletes are sent by their region to compete against each other. Winners are declared the best in the country in their sport or event.

be fast and agile, and all of those traits put into the runway. Then, the take-off area, you need to be as strong as, I don't know, Hidilyn Diaz. Then you need to be as graceful as the gymnasts to feel the pole and be able to align with it and ride it to maximize that energy vertically. How gymnasts train, we have some of that. Then how weightlifters train, we have gym sessions. All of that combined makes pole vaulting one heck of an event that is probably not going to be boring like sprinters just running, running, running. That is how I see pole vaulting. In my programme here in Rome, I train 8–10 times a week, and that 8–10 times a week are all different sessions. I go to the gymnastics area sometimes, and then I go to the track and do some long jumps because I need to work on my takeoff. I have my gym sessions where I need to get strong and be powerful enough to do what I need to do. Combine that all together in my jump, in my vaulting.

JA: Let's talk in terms of the progress and how you actually develop that— that capacity to be able to do that?

EJ: I think the growth spurt definitely helped. But the good thing about pole vaulting, there are numbers, and you would know when you actually improved. In pole vault it's like you're inching your way to that next height. You don't necessarily just get faster. My dad did a lot to help me with which part of pole vaulting I needed to focus on until I was able to reach 5 metres.

On learning from his coach Vitaly Petrov

EJ: My coach Vitaly Petrov said to me, 'Oh, you're jumping 5 metres now. In three months, you're going to jump 5.1, 5.20.'

I remember he said 5.20. I'm just like, 'It took me a year to go from 4.95 to 5 metres and you're telling me in three months I'm going to jump 5.20? You're full of it.' I was just like, 'Yeah. I'm going to follow your training. You're a legendary coach, but I think you didn't understand the work I put in to get to where I'm at.'

In Asia, 5 metres is a decent pole vaulter. And then suddenly, I'm in Europe. I haven't vaulted for six weeks. What is this going to do? I just trusted the process. To be honest, I really didn't have a choice, either. At the time, I didn't say anything. I just said, 'Yes, sir. Yes, coach. Yes, I'll do it.' I went back to the Philippines and had my first competition. I jumped with the new national record, which is 5.01 and set my name in the record sheet of Philippine athletics. The week after, I jump 5.05, and the week after jump 5.15, and the week after jump 5.20, then 5.21 eventually. I'm just like, well, I guess he's right. He knows what he's doing.

On facing challenges and controversy

JA: I know that recently, there have been a lot of controversies in terms of you and our local Philippine Amateur Track and Field Association (PATAFA). That's not something that I want to discuss because that is water under the bridge. I'm just happy that you were able to get past that because quite frankly, that was one of the reasons why I ended my career in track and field back then. I felt that it was hard to make a career out of track and field. I just graduated from Ateneo and at that time, I still tried to compete, still tried to represent the country but after a while I decided that the best next step for me would be to be able to pursue my other passions, which in this case, brought me to the world of media. Because although I did want to represent the country, I ended up right now doing what I do, which is also in a way representing our country but in a totally different arena.

EJ: I'm just curious about the decision that you made, was it worth it for you, that it makes sense now? The moment you decided you wanted to stop, and you wanted to focus on a different passion, was it something that you can just go to bed and really not worry about like it doesn't get into your head any more? It's just something that happened, and I live with it, and it is fine?

JA: You know, EJ, I understand where you're coming from. I know that after the Olympics because of the whole debacle, you did release a statement saying that maybe it was time for you to move on. What I can say? For me, at the time, when I made the decision, it was quite easy. I remember, I was twenty-three years old and representing the country at the Singapore Open. I was training at the time for the chance to be included in the lineup for the Southeast Asian Games. I was competing in the 100-metre dash which really was my first love. I remember the heat that I was in. I finished fifth in my heat and for someone who is used to winning and having all of these records, I was not used to it. At that time, I already had my hand in doing a lot of media work. I was writing, I was producing the news. I had already started my career in media while trying to hold on to the glory days of track and field because I really also wanted to give it another shot. I thought I was young enough that if I did pursue it, I would be able to be perhaps one of, if not the best, sprinter in the Philippines. The Singapore Open ended up being my last competition.

What ended up happening was that the guy who beat me in the 100 metres the year before in the UAAP, Ralph Soguilon, eventually broke the

Philippine record and became the fastest man in the Philippines. Sometimes, I would go back to that and think, was it worth it for me to quit at that time? I could have been the fastest ever in the country.

But EJ, to be honest, I have no regrets. I felt that it was time for me to move on. Whatever successes that I've had in the past, I was very happy and content. I think that's what I can share with you as the turning point for me. That was the time when I felt deep inside that I was ready to move on. I knew that my other passion, which was media, was already calling me. To this day, I tell people that being a former athlete actually prepared me for the next chapter of my life. The next season of my life. The successes and the failures of that time really enabled me to be able to dig deep. When I had to be a struggling entrepreneur, and how to overcome all of these failures in my new career and eventually business. I actually wanted to reach out to you after the Olympics when you said that you were at a crossroads and I just want to say to you, EJ, that at no point in our country's history have we ever had a track athlete as good as you. I think you were put there for a reason.

The next couple of years are going to be important because of what you can potentially be. I don't know how close you are to being number one. But I want you to know that this is the very first time that we actually have a shot. This is the first time that we've ever had a contender. I think you winning a medal, more so if it's a gold medal in track and field, will cement you in the annals of history. The next Olympics is only a few years away. If I were in your shoes, I would exhaust all possible means. I know you have it in you, so I hope that despite all the obstacles that you've had, you'll be able to get past all of this because you're a once-in-a-generation talent. People believe in you. So, I hope that we see you EJ in the next Olympics and bring home the gold.

Fast Talk with John

What makes you Asian and what makes you Filipino?

Just my approach to the training. Now that I've seen, roughly, you know, how the centre of track and field kind of works. Being a Filipino, it's just different. We're just used to being a little bit more . . . I'm not going to say pain but, you know, we just can go a little bit further down that path. When you know you're running the 400, we can just go dig deep, a little bit deeper. And I think that's what makes me a Filipino, and that's something that I'm truly proud of.

Is there anything from the Philippines that you would like for people to know or discover? It could be anything, food, people, places?

Talking to these fellow pole vaulters, it's always the islands. I just said, you know, you should visit the islands. They are beautiful. Diversity, and it's a paradise. It is totally a paradise. The Philippines is a beautiful place.

Who to you is a modern-day superhero. If there is one person, what superpower would this person possess?

Right now, my superhero is my coach. Just the way he approached the game and winning everything that could have been won, and he's still here willing to do the work, and actually push us even more than we push ourselves. It's just a totally different kind of mindset. I guess that mindset makes him my modern-day superhero.

If you could give a commencement speech at the Ateneo. What message would you give to the students out there who know of you, who have heard of you, and who admire you? What would be your message to them as they go into their own respective roles, not necessarily in the field of sports, but in life? What would be your message to them?

Do the best that you could do and put your heart out to the passions that you want to do and keep. Keep doing that because you never know who you're going to inspire. You never realize this until your journey's concluded. It is a different kind of feeling and I think I'm going to give the same little things if you could change the world to make it better. That's the best thing that you can do in this life. That's the same speech I heard when I was in Ateneo. We're meant to change the world to be a better place.

What keeps you up at night and conversely, what gets you up in the morning?

What keeps me up at night is a lot of things. Maybe just, you know, not being able to put everything into training or just overthinking why did I have a bad jump session? Those kinds of things. What gets me up in the morning is just another chance to do it all over again, but a little bit better.

How do you prepare for what you do? Any special routines you can share with us?

Pretty boring. It's become a cycle. It's become a day-to-day routine that I do. I wake up, I prepare my breakfast, I go to the track, I go back home. If I need to do interviews, you know, this mundane schedule of mine. Nothing crazy special, something weird.

Training-wise anything that maybe you would like to share with us?

I think the way I've approached the game is just different now. The way the injury taught me that, you know, in the snap of a finger, my career could be over. Therefore, today might be the last day that I'm doing this. I'm going to give it my all, that's something that I always say and it's written on my door every single day. That is just me. That's maybe the difference in the way I approach my sport.

What do you do in your downtime and how are you able to regain focus? I can imagine there have been so many distractions, the past couple of months or perhaps years, anything that you do to be able to just calm down and regain focus on what you need to do.

I like to run. When I want to calm down, I just go to the track. Put either music or no music at all, just keep running until the point that you don't realize you're running; your mind is the one really running. What I mean is, when running, you're thinking about the things that are bothering you, what are the thoughts in your head, you know, your demons inside you, kind of make peace with them during those times. That's how I recentre. If I cannot run because I have another training session, I try to sit down, just close every electronic device and just start drawing and doing all of this and then, while doing it, I kind of get into that point again where I don't realize I'm drawing. My mind is literally so far away from me. I think that's very crucial for my event, pole vaulting. Having doubts in the poles that I need to use and having doubts on the runway definitely don't help. So just being able to make peace with my inner demons and those kinds of ways to just kind of recentre myself and be calm. It's very important.

What is the one thing you wish you could have known or learned sooner?

I still haven't learned it. I'm still learning it right now. And just to be, you know, just communicate a little bit better. There are always different perspectives and different approaches and things and, sometimes, you kind of put other people in the way. That is not ideal. Maybe I'm still learning it. Things that I wish I had learned earlier. Just to be able to understand. Not just understanding the motivation of why people do what they do. It's just what perspective do they actually have in their certain position that is different from mine?

What would your epitaph say?

'I live a life with no regrets.' That's why I asked you a while ago. That's what I wanted to put on that stone. This was a guy who lived his life with no regrets, which means you know, I did whatever I could do. At the end of the day, whatever the result may be, I'm fine with it.

If there's anything that you do that you would like for me to try or for anyone to try for that matter, what would that be?

Maybe you've tried it: pole vaulting. But what makes me a better pole vaulter, it's actually playing tennis mentally. The stress of it, it's tennis. But I would love to see you vault again. I would love to meet you in person. I'm not kidding because, as I said, I knew your name before I even met you. Before you even reached out to me. I knew because you had the record in high school. A kid that went before me, I guided him—and I wouldn't say I coached him formally but I guided him. We aimed for that record.

My Thoughts

My interview with EJ was by far the most emotional and meaningful I have ever done. In a lot of ways, we are kindred spirits, and what I went through transitioning from being an athlete to establishing a career and eventually a business is one that EJ is currently grappling with.

As of this book's writing, EJ has just won the bronze in the World Athletics Championships, clearing a new personal and Asian record of 5.94 metres. He is currently the third ranked pole vaulter in the world. With the Paris Olympics being only a few years away, EJ is in a good position to make history for the Philippines, which only recently won its first Olympic gold medal through weightlifter Hidilyn Diaz. That gold for Diaz has made her a national hero and has given her earnings from her sport and endorsements far beyond her wildest dreams.

As we wrapped up the interview, EJ expressed to me just how thankful he was for the insights that I shared with him, and I likewise told him of my willingness to be there for him on the sidelines for the next Olympics. I may not have reached the pinnacle of athletic success that he can draw inspiration from, but I have made the right decisions that has made me live a life with no regrets—something that EJ hopes will be the same for him as he endeavours to make history for himself and his country.

Chapter Assignments

Not everyone can be an Olympian, but there are certain things that some successful athletes have done that we can all learn from. EJ has done some things well, but circumstances also made his journey to the Olympics possible. Some food for thought:

- Your coaching needs will change as you progress in your sport. To be really successful, get the best coaching you can. Successful athletes such as EJ, and Venus and Serena Williams started out being coached by their parents, but eventually found the best coaches to take their careers to the next level.

- The advantage of picking an obscure sport or event is that not a lot of people do it. So, assuming you put in the hard work and proper training, the chances of you doing well or ranking high in the percentile of people who do it increases. Consider picking a sport not everyone is into. If you take to it and you do well and enjoy it, you might just get competitive enough to one day be a contender yourself.

- The disadvantage with getting into something that not a lot of people are into is that it's difficult to find a mentor. Find a mentor or at least someone who has gone through what you are going through. In my short but emotional conversation with EJ, we both ended up in tears as EJ found in me someone who could relate to what he is going through. Finding one gives you an emotional anchor beyond the technical support and coaching you need to succeed.

Rovilson Fernandez

TV personality and host
Amazing Race Asia, Asia's Got Talent, Ang Pinaka

**'I love the team sports concept of either winning or
losing but just playing the game right.'**

You might win one day, you might not—but play the odds

*Rovilson Fernandez has put the Philippines on the map by becoming one of the most sought-
after hosts in Asia.*

*Born in Japan to Filipino parents, he was raised in the US, where he lived the first
twenty-six years of his life. In 1999, he moved to the Philippines to start a career in the
entertainment industry.*

If you're into international talent searches, beauty contests, and reality shows, you'll know he has definitely made the rounds.

His buddy Marc Nelson and he made up one of the most memorable teams on The Amazing Race Asia, finishing as one of the finalists on the show's second season.

Years later, the dynamic duo became hosts of Asia's Got Talent.

He has worn many hats as a model, brand ambassador, fitness icon, and a man with never ending punchlines.

On how he began his career in the entertainment industry

I didn't fully immerse myself in the Manila life until I moved when I was twenty-six. I moved because I wanted to do something grand and different and epic before the new millennium. I love Asia and I love the Philippines. I remember watching my mom glued to the TV set and she would watch her favourite Filipino show *Keep on Dancing* every Friday like clockwork. It was then hosted by three guys. I had no intentions yet of moving to the Philippines, but I was just seeing how happy my mom was and she was so lost and engaged. I was like, I want to put that kind of happiness into my mom. I was like, you know, I could do what they're doing. I wanted to be in entertainment at some capacity in the Philippines because it looks like so much fun, and if these three jokers can do it, I can do it.

On auditioning for and competing on The Amazing Race Asia

Out of all the TV shows I've done, that show leaves the biggest dent in my heart. It was my greatest victory, just getting on that show. It was also my worst defeat.

I remember lots of friends and family members would tell us, 'We would watch you guys during dinner', 'The family actually watched TV with *The Amazing Race Asia* going on', and I was so touched by that. That's what I love, a shared family experience.

Marc and I, we said, 'We're already hosts, let's take advantage of that. Let's use our resources in the industry, let's put together a kick-ass audition tape', because in all honesty the real race is the auditions, not the Amazing Race itself. You're only going against eleven other teams. In the audition process, you're going against thousands of teams, so you have to make yourself stand out. That's where we really concentrated. We hired a world-class photographer, we borrowed his studio, he came with a wonderful makeup artist, we had a script. I wrote it, it was inspired by the Apple commercial at the time, it was the 'I'm a PC, I'm a Mac'. Of course, I was the PC and Marc was the Mac. It's one of my finest pieces of work, seriously.

I'll tell you this now, the producer of *The Amazing Race Asia* pulled us aside and said, 'Your audition tape was the best I've ever seen.' It was so worth it because we put in a lot of time and effort. That made us realize, if you do your research, put your work in, put your time in, you will get great returns.

On his work buddy, Marc Nelson

The differences between us were so in sync; it just happened organically, and it was so successful for us. I don't want to say we finish each other's sentences, but we had the same jokes, similar likes, similar dislikes, but also there's a lot of things that we don't get along with. It's just a perfect gelling and matching of two buddies and I think, back in that time, the early 2000s, the buddy formula was just starting. I think we were the first super team host. We were the Miami Heat of hosting. When we're working together, we're riffing off each other. From an economic standpoint, hey you get two hosts for one. It's just been natural, it's cool. I don't know where to go from here. Do we get married? What are we doing next?

On working in Singapore

As much as I love Manila and it plays a huge role in my formation, Singapore is my second home. Career-wise, everything amazing has happened in Singapore. Of course, it's the headquarters for all networks in southeast Asia, if not Asia. I love everybody there, I love the food, I love the culture. But when you work in Singapore, it's on a different level. I would consider it the Hollywood level of Asia. And the greats work there, people from Hollywood or Bollywood or Chinese cinema. It was such an honour to be involved and working closely with the crème de la crème of southeast Asia. You learn things, they have a system, they're much more efficient than we are. I like the Philippines; the working environment is better than theirs. They're a little too serious for me, but to each their own. I feel we're a little more creative, we have more flair, but them they are technically superior, progressive, their advancements in technology and writing are pretty good. It was just a mesh of two worlds. It was such a treat to work in Singapore and we can learn a lot from them, government-wise too.

On loving his job

It's such an honour to do what we do and the fact that we call it work, but it's not even close to work. The quote, do something you love and never work a day in your life, it so rings true for what I've been doing. I'll never be an athlete that will go to the Olympics and represent my country, the Philippines, but how I can best represent being Filipino is doing international work and just killing it on stage.

On competing at Spartan races against guys in tutus

For this section, the exchange between Rovilson and I is just too good and entertaining to pass up, so we go with the verbatim interview as recorded on the podcast, *Methods to Greatness*.

JA: Rovilson, I want to get into the other big part of your life, which is not Marc, but your athletic career. You were never a professional athlete, but you are fit as an ox. You work out like crazy, you've been on the cover of Men's Health rocking that tight fit muscle shirt. I've seen you work, we've competed before in races, and I know just how strong you are as a runner. You're a huge guy but at the same time you have the endurance of a middle-distance runner. You've done a couple of marathons also. What is the secret to staying in shape the way that you are having the lifestyle that you have?

RF: I absolutely just enjoy being out there and getting sweaty. I love the team sports concept of either winning or losing but just playing the game right. Yes, I was never a professional sports player, but I always gave my best and the Beast inspired me.[8] I always tried to race against them. I knew my place, but you know what it's sports, you might win one day, you might not but play the odds. That's what I absolutely love about it. There's no greater time than now that health is so important. And sports, health, wellness, and fitness has also been very good to me financially.

JA: You're, right now, one of the Spartan race ambassadors of the Philippines and you've competed in a couple of really tough races. You don't just do the sprints, you do everything. You do the Beast, you do the Trifecta.[9] For those who don't know much about Spartan racing, give us a

---

[8] A 21 kilometre event of the obstacle course race, Spartan.

[9] The Spartan Trifecta is earned by completing three different Spartan obstacle course races events in one calendar year, usually comprising the 5 kilometre Sprint,

clue what it takes. We've raced together in some but for those who haven't done it, what's it like?

RF: Spartan race is basically an obstacle course set across designated distances, usually 5, 10 kilometres or up to 21 kilometres, three different levels, strewn across certain types of terrain. Some races can be muddy, some races can be up in the hills, some races can be in the desert and that's what's fantastic about that. You are just pitting yourself against nature, you're pitting yourself against your colleagues, your fellow Spartans, and the greatest one is you're pitting yourself against yourself. I know it sounds so cheesy but that is the greatest time to really push yourself. Out of all the sports that I've done and participated in, Spartan is the most fulfilling. It combines a lot of different tasks and body movements and skill sets. It's the greatest parallel to life, where if you don't train hard enough for something you won't be successful in it. You can get by; you can cross the finish line, but if you want to cross the finish line a champ you've got to work for it. It's a great community too. The Spartan community is amazing, it's not just tough guys, it's also executives, mothers, paraplegics, kids. It's a wonderful community, very supportive of each other. There's no arrogance in it and the medals are shiny and heavy and substantial.

JA: I agree totally, 100 per cent, but I think what attracts me to it is that we're both in our forties. Just the fact that you're out there, the sun, the mud, going down not even on your knees, crawling and submerging yourself, there's fire and you've got sweaty people just inching their way trying to make it to the finish line. It makes me feel like I'm still capable of doing this stuff, it's like, I don't know, is it a midlife crisis you think? It just makes you feel like it's something cavemen would do on a daily basis.

RF: It's like you made a fire with your own hands. I totally get what you're feeling. It's so primal, it's so exotic. And I love how some guys, the elite levels, they'll strip down, just running in compression shorts. They're as bare as Tarzan and I'm not that level yet.

JA: And Jane because the women there are tough too. When someone this small passes you and she's not even elite level, she's just really working hard so you, as someone with just even a little bit of pride you will refuse to get passed.

RF: Here's the worst one for me. There are some Spartans out there who are running in multi-coloured tutus, with feather wings like in Victoria's Secret. If

---

10 kilometre Super, and 21 kilometre Beast.

they're in front of me, I'm like *puta*, really? I'm so tired, but I have to at least pass the guy in the tutu. I can't let the guy in the tutu beat me. I remember one time we were doing ultra, which is a 50 kilometre race, and this is in Porac, Pampanga, the hottest, most treacherous place to do a race. I was on my ninth hour of this 10-hour race. I was about to complete it and maybe the last 2 kilometres I was fighting with a guy wearing a multi-coloured tutu, knee-high socks with Powerpuff Girls on it, and I was like, nothing wrong with his outfit I just couldn't let New Balance lose to this guy.

JA: But that's probably part of his strategy as well.

RF: It was a mind game, yes. I barely beat him, but I swear. Finishing the 50 kilometre race in 10 hours was not my greatest victory. My greatest victory was passing that dude in the coloured tutu. We all have our own personal victories and that was mine. But anyway, it's a wonderful, strong, amazing community.

JA: It is and I'm glad to be part of it. After this pandemic, I hope that we do a race together, man.

RF: We should race in tutus and throw mind games with people behind us.

On preparations before a show

We got a good night's rest, that was number one. For *Asia's Got Talent* we had to make sure we rested well because we were on our feet for a long time. It's a physical show, not just script reading, but it was taxing on the body. We always made sure to get a good workout the night before. We always knew that it just helped blood flow into the parts that need blood, and you feel better, you feel lighter. We made it a point to wake up 2 hours earlier than call time and just go through the script. You're only as good and talented as your knowledge of the script. If you know the script, you can go in any direction you want and put in your own personal flavor. And, of course, we always had fun.

On worrying

I've learned that you shouldn't worry about things you can't control. Deal with it when you have to, cross that bridge when you get there. I'm very big on being in the now, in the moment. Don't think about the past, no regrets. Plan a bit for the future but be in the moment now.

Fast Talk with John

What makes you Asian, specifically what makes you Filipino?

My love for rice. No, I'm just kidding. Filipinos are different in the way we look. We all have different cultures, dialects, so for me the Filipino is a state of mind. That's what makes me Filipino, it's my heart. It's my attitude and my love for the Philippines.

What is it about the country, whether it's the food, the culture, or customs that you would love for people outside the country or outside of Asia to discover?

You need to come here; you have to stand on our soil. Our hospitality is different, our food is different, the camaraderie, the love, the friendship. They need to come here and go to any island with white sand and have a boodle fight set up for them. A boodle fight is basically banana leaves spread out on a table, rice will be the foundation and around that rice you'll have *liempo* or grilled pork, shrimps, mangoes, cucumber salad, chicken *inasal*, pork. You'll have an amazing barbecued feast in front of you and here's the killer part— no utensils. You have to eat with your hands. All of you gather around it and boom, you just eat with your hands. The food will be amazing, the ambience will be amazing, but it's the camaraderie of eating side by side with Pinoys that is just *iba*. You can't get that anywhere else.

Who to you is a modern-day hero and what qualities does this person have that makes him or her your hero?

I'll choose two locally that are just so profound. First and foremost, Maria Ressa of Rappler. Do I even need to go into what she's going through? Just a strong, amazing, smart woman going up against the forces of evil. Anyone lesser would have crumbled by now but she's still staying strong and vigilant.

The second person I'd like to bring up is Gina Lopez, rest in peace. She's the type of person that not only talks the talk, she walks the walk. I've had the pleasure and honour of protesting alongside her and she's just so charismatic.

I miss Miriam Defensor Santiago, she's the greatest president we never had, I will say that outright. Not to get into politics but those three are wonderful icons.

Of course, our parents. It's such a cliché to say our parents were heroes to all of us individually but they really are the ones that were there for us.

They really are our rocks in whatever way. I love all parents especially at this age now.

I don't know if you've given a commencement speech but if given the chance, what is the message that you would like to give people who are coming into the real world who have this ideal of what it's like to be out there?

The one thing that I learned looking back that got me to where I am now is I believed in myself. I invested in myself. I said, I have to take care of my brand. Reputations are not built overnight. Believe in yourself, believe in your brand. It's okay to watch others who you admire but you also have to remember to put in your personal flavor.

What is the one thing that you wish you could have known or learned sooner that is now helping you navigate your career or your life now?

I wish I saved a lot more when I was younger and made wiser investments. I didn't, and I'm telling you all now, save and make wise investments. Real estate is great, stocks are fantastic. Stay away from restaurants and bars unless you have a lot of money. That's from a financial standpoint. From a spiritual and personal standpoint, I'm quite happy with the path I took but I wish I stayed in touch with friends more.

If someone were to follow in your footsteps, what would be the best advice that you could give to that person?

Don't burn your bridges. Be nice and kind to everyone, including crew, because you never know if they're going to be the directors and the producers that will be hiring in the future. You don't want to step on any toes and make enemies. Believe in yourself, that's the absolute game changer. If they're just starting out, get as many rounds in as possible. Get those gigs that you don't want to get, those P22,000 gigs hosting a launch of a detergent or your friend's baptism reception. Keep doing it, keep working on your craft. Just do it because you love it.

What would your epitaph say?

I'm sorry, I'm late. I'm always late, I might as well put that on the tombstone. People be like, 'Typical Rovilson, late for his own funeral.' Just to crack one last joke. And a fist bump, a mould of my hand in cement so that when you come to visit me, you see my line and then you fist bump me.

Is there anything that you would recommend that you do in your life that I or any other person can try that you were successful in doing or achieving in the past?

I recommend, especially now, people must get their personal advocacy, whatever it is. Health, wellness, good governance, climate change, animal welfare, human rights, whatever your passion is. Get that one advocacy and protect it. Be passionate about it. Promote it, create awareness.

I have several that I'm very passionate about. Climate change of course is very important to me. Children, the deaf community is something very close to my heart. Pour as much of your free time into it as possible. People think you have to be a celebrity, or you have to be famous, or you have to have thousands of millions or thousands of followers. No. Everybody has a platform. If you have five friends on social media, you have a platform.

My Thoughts

Rovilson is a guy's guy and is one of the kindest and overall great human beings I know. He carves an imposing figure with his Men's Health Magazine cover body but is really a marshmallow deep inside.

He may not be a professional athlete, but he has exemplified the discipline and consistency it takes to be fit way into his forties that keeps him in top form that extends to his profession. There is a lot to learn from how Rovilson makes working out part of his routine as a professional host.

I believe 100 per cent in making exercise an integral part of one's regimen no matter what profession you're in. But beyond that, what Rovilson and I found is that competing in obstacle races such as Spartan is something that brings us to a place where we can have a competitive outlet. I believe sports competitions such as races can bring out the best and worst in people. If you're the former, it allows you to set goals you can achieve either for yourself or as a way to benchmark against other people. Call it midlife crisis if you will, but these races allow for people to bring out the best in themselves.

Rovilson also talked about investing in himself through the years and taking care of his brand. This paved the way for a long and fruitful TV career spanning decades. He is a classic case of someone believing in himself and his capabilities, and this belief reflected in his lifestyle and how he approaches his mind and body.

Chapter Assignments

Armed with a passion for his craft, Rovilson went to the Philippines in the hopes of starting a career in the entertainment industry. Over two decades since, he has become one of the most talented and sought after hosts not just in the country but all over Asia. He takes care of his reputation as much as he takes care of his body as a professional host, leading to his prolific career. You too can achieve longevity by considering a change in your path or taking on something new:

- Take risks. If you find yourself stuck in a rut, try something else. Get a new job, go into another venture, travel, get out of your comfort zone. If you have family or connections in another country, discover your roots and move there. Like Rovilson, you might just find yourself living another life you never could have begun to imagine.
- Be passionate about something and take to advocacy. Whatever it is—health, wellness, good governance, climate change, animal welfare, human rights—make time for it and make yourself and the world a better place.
- Be kind—to your body, and to other people. This seems to be something Rovilson takes to naturally. Eat healthy, stay fit, and treat everyone with the same respect they deserve. Your body and other people will thank you for it.

Chien Han How

Medical entrepreneur
Founder of Sleepwake Centre and Singapore Robotics Centre

**'Do not be so tense, so stressed out all the time.
Learn to let go of certain things.'**

Sleep and age better

A firm believer in the use of technology to enhance the diagnosis, treatment and monitoring of patients, Chien Han How has close to thirty years of experience in managing a business that supports the management of patients with neurophysiological, respiratory, and sleep disorder conditions.

His interest in medical entrepreneurship was influenced by the time he served in the army as a medic for two and a half years. After finishing his service, he joined a company that sold sleep equipment. Eventually, Chien pursued his own business goals and founded the Sleepwake Centre, which helps adults and children resolve various sleep disorders.

One of Sleepwake Centre's innovations is the 'on-the-go' portable sleep diagnostics programme, which Chien developed, where patients can be monitored for their sleep disorders outside a hospital or clinic setting.

As an entrepreneur, Chien has realized that many patients are either not aware of technology to aid them or think that technological devices are expensive and out of reach. Chien wants to change that. He wants to make technology more accessible to more patients who can benefit from it—and he found that one of the ways to do so is through the use of robotics in rehabilitation. By setting up the Singapore Robotics Centre, Chien hopes to bring rehabilitation or physiotherapy to the next level.

Chien believes that no patient should be deprived of technology that can improve their chances of recovery. He believes that technology has a big role to play in developing the rehabilitation landscape, where efficiency and efficacy are key.

On the importance of good quality sleep

About one-third of our life is spent sleeping. Having good quality sleep means you can perform better in the day at work or during family time, or whatever. I don't only look at obstructive sleep apnea, actually, in a professional sleep centre because you look at other disorders; there are over forty classified sleep disorders, like sleep walking, night terrors.

I think the amount of sleep varies from person to person, but the research has shown that you need at least six to eight hours of sleep to perform well in the day. If you don't get that, then the energy level is not there. And in sleep, our body recuperates, especially for children. The growth hormones kick in during sleep.

Sleep hygiene is about timing yourself so that you gradually get used to sleeping at the same time and you wake up at the same time. It's important also to relax yourself and not to eat so much before you sleep.

Do not be so tense, so stressed out all the time as well. Learn to let go of certain things sometimes.

On treating one of the most common sleep disorders: sleep apnea

The first line of treatment for sleep apnea now is actually using a breathing machine called CPAP, which stands for continuous positive airway pressure. So, it's basically like wearing a face mask, a nasal mask that's connected to a machine, which is like a blower, a vacuum cleaner in reverse. It gives you a continuous flow of air to split open the airway, so that the airway has no chance to collapse, and you can have regular non interrupted breathing.

The design of this machine is to enable patients to bring it back home to use every night. It is smaller, the mask is more comfortable, more easy to put on. You can use it overnight, and the noise level is very low. Actually, the design of it makes it more and more easy to use now but it's still a challenge, I would say, for many people because you have been sleeping without anything on your face, and now you have to put this thing on. So, I think part of our job for the sleep centre is to motivate and to encourage people to use it. We can monitor it through a cloud-based system where we can see how they breathe, how they use it, and how many hours they use. So, this is also an important factor to make them more compliant.

On the unconventional method of hypnosis for a good night's sleep

I actually practiced clinical hypnosis before. We would go through scripts on relaxation, like a gardening script, where you are just walking in the garden and you see all sorts of flowers, and the trees and all that. So, it's not a very exciting sort of thing, but it's like a rhythm, a very monotonous rhythm that actually helps to relax you.

For example: you walk into a garden. You see a gate, and while you pass through that gate, you will see a sea of greenery. Below you is the green, green grass. And you see trees being shaken by the wind that is blowing through. It sounds cheesy but by hearing it calms you down already. Voice is also important.

You can customize it as well to suit your interests. It's something like daydreaming. For me, it's going to the beach, listening to the sea, feeling the breeze blowing on your face and all that.

On the ease of using new sleep technologies

The conventional policy used to be to have sleep tests done only in a hospital setting. It would be in a big room where you have all the gadgets and camera videos and then you need to link it to another room, which is the computer room where the technologies will be there to monitor for the test for the whole night. So, my strength is actually to make it so I'm able to pack it all in a suitcase, and bring it to wherever the patient can sleep, and then set up the cameras and the equipment and all that to conduct this test.

On addressing geriatric medical problems through robotics

I think the ageing population has many problems with regards to movement. We are very much focused, through our robotics, on the areas of neurology and recovery from diseases like stroke. I think there is a big role for robotics to play, and we need to have people who can facilitate this. So having more rehab centres, I think, really helps and then we need to have people drive these rehab centres.

Using robotics is important also for the therapist doing it. I think you also need to give them a sense of ease when doing their therapy, because the conventional ways of doing physiotherapy can be very labour-intensive. It is very strenuous. Every year, there are a lot of therapists who experience burnout, and there's burnout from the patient's side too because it's very frustrating. So why not make use of technology, make use of robotics equipment, to make everyone's life easier?

We use an exoskeleton, and this technology is actually not new. It's actually from the US Army. They will design all these robotics links and all that for soldiers to run faster and to carry more. And then they built interesting games into it as well so that when the patients are doing therapy, they are in augmented reality and virtual reality. It makes the whole process fun and motivates them to do more.

There's a treadmill, and in front of it, there's a screen with virtual reality. And then you have the augmented reality where on the treadmill itself, there are projections of obstacle courses where the patient has to go through. So, it's a combination of both. For the exoskeleton, it actually fits onto a treadmill, which has a hoist for body support that prevents patients from falling.

Setting up maybe needs a bit of time, but it's so much easier than just conventional therapy, of supporting yourself and then getting a therapist to hold on to you. They have all these harnesses and straps to hoist you up. In conventional therapy, you might take just a few steps, even two or three steps, and it would be so tedious. With this robotics equipment, you can go up to hundreds of steps within a short amount of time.

During the opening of our centre, we actually got a friend's dad who actually suffered from brain injury. Half of his head is actually gone, it's all soft tissue without the scalp. And I remember my friend actually told me that he was given a death sentence like there was no hope from the doctors. Our friend knew about this robotics and insisted on doing it, and now the dad can actually take a few steps, and I think that is really remarkable in the sense that even the medical experts thought that it cannot be done. So, I think that therein lies the hope that we can see.

Fast Talk with John

What makes you Asian? Specifically, what makes you Singaporean?

Asia is a very versatile, very flexible, fast-moving economy, so I think everything we do in Asia is fast, fast, fast, and efficient—trying to get everything done as soon as possible.

Is there anything from your country (food, place, custom) that you would like the world to know about or discover?

Singapore is very multiracial. So you can find all sorts of food and culture, and it's a highly cultural mix here, so if you want to know more about Asia, Singapore is a place where you can go. I am involved in Beijing opera and comedy dialogue; we call it crosstalk in Chinese. There is what we call the Artistic Club, an opera company I go to. Chinatown is always the place for Chinese culture, and the club is actually located there.

Who, to you, is a modern-day superhero?

My version of what you call a superhero, essentially, are the unsung heroes, which I find are people who are not really well-known in our society, but they are like superheroes to me. Even the ones that are sweeping the road, for example. He can be very focused and very committed to his job. And I think, to me, this is like a superhero because he wants to do his job well.

What keeps you up at night?

Sometimes I can be very deep in thought about my work, and about my family, too.

What is the one thing you wish you could have known or learned sooner?

The importance of having a mentor, of knowing the right people who can show me the ropes of life.

If there is anything specific you do that you would recommend I try, what would it be?

Try to hypnotize yourself. Try hypnosis to calm yourself down. Don't always to be so fast-paced. Learn to let go. I think that there's a Chinese saying that if you were to grab a handful of sand, the tighter you grip the sand, the more sand will leak out from your fingers. So, I think that concept is very similar. So, it's like, you must learn to let go sometimes to relax.

My Thoughts

These days, I make sure I get between seven to eight hours of sleep a night. It used to be really bad—particularly at the height of the pandemic when anxiety and stress levels were so high and I would get maybe five hours a night.

The way I've regulated this is to make sure to not do any kind of work on my laptop or any kind of heavy thinking after dinner. The perfect routine would be a sauna bath after my afternoon workout, cold shower, dinner at 6 p.m., some mindless TV watching and snuggling time with my wife and seven-year-old boy, dim lights, hot chamomile tea, and shuteye by 10 or 11 p.m. Since we don't have blackout blinds, I've resorted to wearing an eye patch, which I've found to be truly one of the most helpful hacks I've picked up that enables me to stay asleep longer in the morning.

Good sound sleep really is the foundation for health and affects everything you do. The days I don't sleep enough I know and feel I am not at my optimal self, so I make sure that I get enough of it.

Chapter Assignments

For many people, a good night's sleep is the ultimate dream, especially when one leads a very busy lifestyle. A relaxing pre-bedtime routine could do the trick—if you make the time for it. Try these simple steps to ensure that you get enough rest at night and be energized throughout the day:

- Wind down an hour before bedtime. Don't just hop into bed when your adrenaline is still up—have a hot shower, read a book, or, like Chien, do some self-hypnosis and picture yourself in the most relaxing setting you can think of.

- Place your gadgets out of arm's reach. This is recommended even by doctors, since the blue light that these devices emit can trick your brain into thinking that it's daytime.
- Say thank you. As you close your eyes, remind yourself of all the things you are grateful for. It's a nice way to usher yourself to the end of the day, and the beginning of a new one.

Chot Reyes

National basketball team coach, TV network CEO, agile mentor

'Great athletes are blessed with a natural ability, but the winners, they're the ones with the inner drive. The reason they are winners is because they are internally motivated.'

What is your why, your purpose, your reason for wanting something?

Chot Reyes is a legend in Philippine basketball.

He is an eight-time Philippine Basketball Association (PBA) champion, five-time coach of the year, seven-time all-star game head coach, and most notably has guided the

Philippine national basketball team, Gilas Pilipinas, to a historic run at the International Basketball Federation (FIBA) World Cup in 2014 after almost forty years.

Apart from being a legendary basketball coach, he headed broadcast network, TV5 as president and CEO from 2016–19.

He has also founded his own company Coachcom, which provides business, teambuilding, leadership development, and agile coaching services.

On what makes winners and motivation

I found that great athletes, they're blessed with a natural ability, but the winners, they're the ones with the ability and inner drive. The reason that they are winners is they are internally motivated. They need somebody to put the programme, maybe somebody to rein them in, but that's the difference.

Even in my work with executives and leaders in other organizations, I always tell them, motivation is overrated. Leaders cannot really motivate their people because real motivation is within, so the only one who can really motivate oneself is yourself. The thing we can do as leaders is to make sure that the environment and the surroundings are conducive for them to get their work done, and then their motivation kicks in. I'm a firm believer that motivation really is about autonomy, mastery, and purpose.

Now I get the question all the time: how can we motivate the millennials and the Gen Z today? The answer is because we're trying to motivate them the way we were motivated, it no longer works. What they want now is autonomy, mastery, purpose. They want to know that they can steer their own ship, they steer it well, and they steer it for a purpose larger than themselves.

What is your why, your purpose, your inner reason for wanting something? There has to be something bigger.

In Gilas, my number one responsibility is to create strong individual relationships with my players because by doing so, I understand what's important to them, what drives them, what are their hot buttons. Those are the things that I use to motivate them. More than motivation, I like to call it inspiration. My job is to inspire them. Those who were less fortunate, they wanted to get to the PBA to improve their lives, for livelihood. But other than that, what's going to take them now to the next level?

On being a student athlete going corporate

I was playing all the way from elementary. I started in the soccer varsity and then it became basketball. In high school, I made the varsity again for UAAP at the same time I made the track and field team. I could have made the soccer team as well. I was athlete of the year, so it was a question of wanting something and being willing to make the sacrifices to make it happen. Very early we learned as athletes to prioritize, to manage our time, to understand the value of rest, recovery. While I was in college, I was, again, in the varsity, that's when my son Josh came. I was only in my second year of college, nineteen years old, so I was a working student. I was working and studying and coaching to augment my income. Those were two very tough years; but I got through it, I graduated on time.

When I graduated, I had an offer to play for the then Philippine Amateur Basketball League (PABL), which is now like the D-League. But I also had an offer to continue working for the company with which I was already working. The salary was the same so, weighing things, I already had a kid, I thought the longer term, better option was to go into corporate work, so I said no to the basketball offers.

A few years later, the company I was working with, Purefoods Corp., decided to enter the PABL. That's how it began. We put together the PABL team of Purefoods. After two years, there was an opportunity because the YCO-Tanduay franchise was disbanding, and they offered it to us. That was my first project: to do a feasibility study on the value of entering the PBA, and so we did; we entered the PBA. But again, I was an executive, I wasn't part of the coaching staff or the management staff of the team.

On changing strategies

When I came to Talk N Text, the last team I coached, very objectively, I told the owners, 'We have too much talent.' And they said, 'What?' I think we were the highest paid in the entire PBA, but in Talk N Text's ten-year existence or so before I arrived, they had won a grand total of one championship and that was kind of a special tournament. I remember the first night that Chairman Manuel V. Pangilinan (MVP) and Ricky Vargas spoke to me, they asked me, 'With the lineup now, can you take us to the finals?' I told them, 'Yes, in one year I can take this team to the finals.' Before I went to the meeting, I already took a look at their roster and did an analysis of the other rosters in the league. One of the first things we did was, if it were even possible, we decreased our level of talent because there's such a thing as getting too talented.

So fortunately, it happened before my first year was up with Talk N Text and we did take the team to the finals, and we won a championship in that first year. It was the same thing with the national team when they appointed me

Gilas coach. I already had a chance in 2007, we didn't do well in Tokushima, and then I retired from the PBA in 2012. But MVP asked me to stay a couple more years. I had retired from the PBA because at fifty, it was time for me to do other things. It was already twenty years in the PBA. Because I didn't have a good experience in 2007, after much thought and consultation with my family, with my wife, we said yes. Again, we began with a very honest assessment of the programme and the assessment was, 'What we are doing now is not working, so are you willing to do things differently?' Now if you apply it to work or a startup or business or a company, it's the same thing. When I took over TV5, I had to begin with a brutally honest assessment of our situation. That assessment meant we cannot bang heads against the two giants. It's no use.

It's public knowledge TV5 was bleeding profusely. There's no way to get out of this situation unless we do things differently. I said we couldn't compete with the two in there because what I learned in sports is you cannot play the other team in their area of strength. You have to find an area where you can win. So that drove the decision to reposition and pivot from being a general entertainment network to a sports network. The only one place that we could win was in sports and digital. I think even before the other two, TV5 was the first to dip its toes into digital because we were willing to disrupt ourselves. Obviously, the two were not because their bread and butter was television broadcast.

So, five years ago we were already producing content for digital only. We were the first to show the Dota E-Sports World Championships. We were pioneers. Now everyone's talking about e-sports, everyone's doing digital.

I believe that what we did then, the most important thing we did was we stopped the bleeding and that allowed us to do several things. We were able to renew our franchise for another twenty-five years, we were able to sign another collective bargaining agreement (CBA), and we were able to do at least a lot of the fundamentals. Now they're able to do a lot of things. What TV5 is doing now is no credit to me at all, it's now under the new management. But I thought where we were in 2016, I think it all began with that very clear understanding of what the problem was and what is the potential solution.

We did that partnership with Entertainment and Sports Programming Network (ESPN) and it allowed us to cut our programming costs drastically, because to be able to produce content for a TV network operating on 16 hours a day is very expensive and the cost of the partnership with ESPN at the time was 50 per cent of that cost. However, it put us in a completely different genre as we were no longer general entertainment and that means that we had access to a much smaller slice of the advertising pie. Much less advertising revenue but much less expense as well. We were able to improve our bottom line significantly in our first couple of years.

On working with his boss, team owner MVP

It was one of the best, if not the best, situations I could find myself in as a coach. He's the kind of ideal owner who understands the game, they understand sports, they know the dynamics, and they put in the resources behind you. They give you whatever you need to win, and they don't interfere; they let you do your job. Yes, they'll call you for meetings and he'll ask why you did this, why that happened, and so on and so forth. But for me that's just natural. He owns the team and all he wanted was to understand that you have a plan and what your plan is. If you could justify it, then it's fine. He hates losing. For him, there's no such thing as a good loss. For him, a loss is a loss.

As a coach, that's all you'd ever ask for. As a coach, what you want is an owner who is going to put his full resources behind you and allow you to coach the way you see fit. That's the situation that I have with MVP. It was the same thing with running a business. In our time in TV5, very few people know this, but we were close to just getting shut down when the losses were just getting to be insurmountable. And, of course, there was the question—whether I was fit to lead the company or not. I was the head of sports, media, and sales, and our CEO quit at the time. So, I was just interim CEO but eventually they made it official. As you will imagine, there were a lot of questions, but MVP came in and gave me his support and so did the board. Again, as an executive, that's all you can ask for; that you get the support, and they allow you to run it the way you see fit.

MVP has a simple, straightforward, powerful take on leadership. For him, leadership is about competence, integrity, and passion. The most important thing is passion. That's why I developed that *puso* framework of leadership, the heart of a leader model. It's about engaging the hearts of your people. For me, that's what leadership is about.

On playing 'small ball'

If you know me as a coach, that's how I coach the game. We do things that are out of the ordinary. So, people talk about 'small ball' that was made popular by the Golden State Warriors in the NBA. Towards their championship runs, they did it with no dominant centre, no top 7-footer, they called it small ball in 2016 or 2017. But people forget we were doing that in Gilas in 2013, 2014 and we were getting all sorts of bashing for it. Why are we playing two small point guards, why do we have three little guys on the court? It wasn't because I wanted to play small ball; it was because I was always doing things that were constantly throwing the other teams off balance.

You can call it unorthodox, out of the box, but for me it was very simple. I just wanted to make sure that if you're the favourite and I'm the challenger and I'm the underdog, I'll be damned if I'm going to do things your way. For example, we try to play the Americans, and we go in with an American style of play, you cannot out-America America. Or you go to Europe, play the European teams, and try a European style of play. You're not going to out-Europe the Europeans. So, we crafted our own Filipino style of basketball. That's Gilas basketball. It's not too scientific, it wasn't always pretty, but we would never give up, we would never quit. We were a very resilient bunch.

On coaching corporates

When I started coaching and I won with Purefoods, I started getting invited to give these corporate talks, motivational talks. I had no idea what to talk about and they told me, 'Just tell us the story of how you won that championship.' So, I did. I talked about the lessons that I learned from that. To my surprise, it was so well received. It's a very different environment but it was kind of very natural. I wasn't trying to teach or preach or train, I was just telling stories. It turns out that was a refreshing thing for the audience to hear. I started getting more and more invites to do these talks. I thought I was kind of like a management consultant, so that's when I decided to take my MBA from the Edinburgh Business School. That's where I found executive and corporate coaching and that spoke to me, to who I am as a person.

So, from the management consultant I said, this is what I want, I want to be a coach. I put up the company Coachcom. I came across John Maxwell; I got accredited as a John Maxwell teambuilder. Then I started getting gigs for team building for organizations. But we got so many inquiries, and we kept saying no because I was still coaching full-time, so we put down the website. It was embarrassing to always say no. It was on and off until, when I was retiring at fifty from basketball coaching, I was really looking towards that. When I finally retired from TV5, it was because I was going to Coachcom full-time, and we were going to expand. I wanted to devote my full time and my efforts towards that.

Of course, we got hit by this pandemic, which is funny because all my talks in the third, fourth quarter of 2019, I always ended it by saying, 'Mark my words we will all be disrupted. It's not a matter of if but it's only a question of when.' Little did I know that we would be disrupted by this virus.

When I retired from TV5, I started asking my clients, 'What are the things that you're grappling with? What are the things that you're interested in?', and they were talking about agility. Agile was top of mind for everyone; it was about resilience, emotional intelligence. I went and took my certification in Singapore to be an agile leadership and management coach. When the pandemic hit, the business got really affected because a lot of my teambuilding gigs—we had a full schedule from February all the way to June—went out the window. We kind of struggled at first but then, little by little, I reached out to my previous clients. They said, 'Coach, can you talk to our people about resilience, how to cope with this thing, because they're all worried.' So, the virtual talks, I was just offering it for free. We figured out a good format for a 35, 40-minute talk, 20 minutes for Q&A. It's been very fun; the talks are about agility, resilience, emotional intelligence, leading in crisis, leadership in times of uncertainty.

On being a leader

Now, because people are looking forward as we're coming out of the pandemic, they're again thinking of teams. The Heart and Science of Great Teams is a talk and a programme that I'm running that I think is very helpful because there's no place for you to go to learn about teamwork and yet anyone, whether you're a startup or an executive or you're running a business, everyone expects you as a leader to run your organization as a well-oiled machine or a good functioning team. Our schools never taught the fundamentals of teamwork, there's no team building. That's where we come in. Even my HEART is an acronym for health, emotional intelligence, agility, resilience and teamwork or teamsmanship. More than the know-how, can they coach you?

I think the most important thing is to remember that even in this virtual time, the value of trust becomes more critical. The leaders today have to take into account: how do I continue building that trust level with my direct reports, with the people under me? There are several ways that we teach that, but the most important thing is when you have meetings, you have to make sure that the first thing you do is don't jump into the agenda first. You have to make sure that you ask them how they are doing. Make sure you're able to connect and show up authentically. For me, authenticity is honesty without self-righteousness. And vulnerability, you have to be very vulnerable. If you're feeling something, if you're worried, don't be afraid to share it as well.

We all know work-life balance, but a lot of leaders are deficient in work-leadership balance. As leaders, we are preoccupied with the work part—analysis, business decision, strategy, and all that—but we forget the leadership part. Listening, putting ourselves in their position, empathy, and all those other things. When you're an individual contributor it's all about your skills and what you can call the work, but as you get promoted that balance starts to tilt. It's less about your skills and more about your leadership. The leader is the emotional beacon, if you will. That's why for me, my number one rule is first, be self-motivated.

On winning your mornings

There's a mistaken 'macho' notion that sleep is for wimps, but the key is if you get up at 5 a.m., you should be ready to sleep at 10 or 11 p.m. I am up at 5 or 5:30 because I have my regular morning routine. Sometimes 4:30 if I need to do something.

First thing I do as soon as I open my eyes, I say thanks right away; thank you nothing happened to me that night, then I do a little stretching routine while I'm still lying down. I get up and I have a glass of water. Then, I go and brush my teeth with my left hand. I learned this from Jim Kwik. When you brush your teeth with your off hand, you're practicing your mind to focus.

Then, I go to my office and do my breathing. I have a 10, 15-minute breathing protocol. It's very simple: just stay seated, feet on the floor, make sure you're breathing the right way—when you inhale, it's your stomach that is expanding. I inhale for four counts, exhale for six counts, then I hold my breath for two counts, and then I inhale again. That's 12 seconds. I do five cycles of that so that's one minute and I do 10, 15 minutes of that. When you exhale more than you inhale, it activates your parasympathetic nervous system, that's the relaxing part. I'm creating space for myself to be relaxed and centred. Then, breakfast at about 7:30 or 8 with my wife.

I do my breathing exercise, meditation, a bit of writing before I even open my email, before I even take a look at my phone. I don't look at this until breakfast time. The worst thing you can do when you wake up is to look at your phone. My belief is, to be successful, you have to have a habit of winning. Win your mornings first. That's something that's completely in your control.

I've been doing yoga sporadically in the past, but during the pandemic, more regularly. I also go and do HIIT, some kind of exercise, or road work, a 5K run-jog-walk-sprint. There's an incline in our village, I sprint up and down five times. It's a combination of a nature walk for me to go out, have sun, and just appreciate nature, because I also teach that in my talks. You have to go out and appreciate it; start from a place of gratitude. One of the ways to be grateful is to go out and appreciate nature.

Especially at my age, I tell people, who cannot do a 5, 10, 15-minute walk? I posted a story about a classmate. We talked about his exercise regimen, everything that he needs to get him out of his wheelchair because he just had his lower legs amputated. I'm saying here is a guy who has no legs and he's concerned about his physical fitness regimen, so what's your excuse?

Then, I get some work done. I get all of those things done and it's not even lunchtime yet. That's what I like doing, what gets me up every day. I pride myself in doing more things than the regular person would be able to do in a day.

On being a supportive father to his athlete-child

I've always believed that while we encourage our children to go into sports or whatever it is that they want, I'm very careful not to be overly involved and to keep a certain distance because we want them to pave their own paths and achieve things on their own merit. But I make sure to give my full support not only to Josh but all our other kids. I wanted to make sure that he stays motivated, that I didn't get in the way, and there was nothing else that was getting in the way. When I knew that he had a competition or a meet coming up, we made sure everything was fine, he had his food, he had enough sleep.

Fast Talk with John

What makes you Asian or in particular what makes you Filipino?

I think my eyes make me unmistakably Asian and my nose makes me Filipino. Other than that, I think about my preference for food. I'm a huge Filipino food junkie but I'm also a huge Asian, southeast Asian food junkie. *Sinigang*, it's a kind of sour broth soup with beef, it can be fish or shrimp, a lot of veggies in there, and it is made with tamarind, with a steaming bowl of white rice.

What makes me Filipino is that I love eating my bread, dip it in coffee, and I put coffee on my fried rice. Coffee with cream, with smoked beef or fish, and then you take the coffee like soup.

To you who is a modern-day superhero, or what qualities would this person have for you to consider them a modern-day superhero?

We talked about him earlier, MVP. I think not only because of his business acumen but being able to work up close and personal with him, I've seen how much he really cares for our country. A lot of the things he does, whether it's increasing the number of hospital beds, improving the road network or water facilities, electricity, is really meant to help the plight of the Filipino. For me it's using your business acumen and resources for the good of others.

That's also what drove my desire to have a dialysis business, to be able to help. Our dialysis business is for the lower income market; we're not going after the high-income patients.

If you were to give a commencement speech, what would be your advice to students who are graduating now at this very challenging time? What is the one advice that you could give them that will help them navigate this new world that we now find ourselves in?

Very simple: don't ever, ever, ever give up. In the same breath, I'll tell them, it's not about you. So go out and have fun. Don't take yourself too seriously.

What keeps you up at night and what gets you up in the morning? Is there something that you feel you still need to do or accomplish?

If there's something that keeps me up at night, it's always the thought that there's something that I still need to do. During this pandemic, what keeps me up really is, both me and my wife, we're constantly worried about our people. We hope that we can continue running the business so that our people will continue to have their livelihood.

What gets me up in the morning is just the excitement of what the day has in store for me. I'm a strong believer in a growth mindset and I'm constantly learning, trying new things, or stretching myself.

What is the one thing that you wish you would have learned sooner in life?

Self-restraint, I guess. I think I have said some things and some hurtful words to some people that I wish I never had. I may have been right, I may have been justified to do it, but still; I always think that it's better if I did not say it.

What would you like for your epitaph to say?

'Here lies a father, a husband, a son, a brother, a friend, a coach, a winner. He made others' lives better.' I think something as simple as that.

If there's one thing that you recommend I try, what is it?

I think the one thing peculiar to my situation, that very few people have gone through, is, yes, I've been widely celebrated but I've also been widely vilified and hated. Getting in that position and surviving it teaches you a lot about yourself. The past five years were really a huge test for me; that I was running a network, I was doing my business, I was still an entrepreneur, I was still giving talks, and I was coaching the national team. That combination of pressures, stress, demands, it really moulds you. You're either going to get better or you're going to break. So that's my challenge to you. The fact is, yes, I've been successful, but I've also failed a lot, but I'm still here to talk to you about the experiences. I've survived it.

I think the most important thing is your purpose. It's got to be something that you really love doing. It's got to be worth it. Otherwise, I would suggest just sticking to your lane. I think the principle of abundance is, it shouldn't be an and/or but you must really know why you're doing it.

My Thoughts

I first met coach Chot Reyes when he used to go with his son Josh, who was in high school at the time, to the track meets. I was in college competing for the same school, Ateneo, and I was curious since Chot was already quite well known at the time, and the same passion he had for coaching was visible as he cheered his son on from the sidelines. That was about a quarter of a century ago, and it makes me realize now, with my own son, that same Chot is now me.

As my seven-year-old David now gets into sports, and being a former successful athlete myself, I have, at least in my imagination, already placed huge pressure on him to do extremely well in athletics. I had him take soccer classes at five years old and he has just gone through a summer of swimming lessons. I also made him train for and compete in his very first Spartan Kids, a 1.6 kilometre obstacle race inside a stadium. One thing that I felt at his age I should instill is to just enjoy the sports he engages in, pretty much like any other game he would play.

I remember when I was eleven years old, my own father introduced me to tennis. He took me to all the clinics and the tournaments, but if there was one thing that I noticed, is that most of the kids I encountered in tournaments were considerably better than me since they took up the sport much younger, some as young as five or seven. For a number of years, I was trying to play catch up, and I felt I could have been better had I acquired the skills earlier. Five years later, when I joined the track team, and because of my foundation with tennis, I found much faster progress because track and field relied on natural athletic ability and physicality, of which I was naturally gifted with.

I remember my dad would get frustrated with my tennis but, later on in high school, just allowed me to blossom as a track athlete under the tutelage of my coach. I would have imagined that my father played a similar role as did coach Chot. Watching from the sidelines, while I figured things out on my own.

As I do the same with David, I only hope that I am able to guide him well without being too strong a presence that he will not find his own identity. I just signed us up and David and I are competing in a Spartan race in two months. I intend not to train him but to train with him. We'll have separate coaches. But he'll know that I'll be right there, working my ass off and leading by example.

Chapter Assignments

According to Coach Chot, what makes winners is motivation, which is about autonomy, mastery, and purpose. Only you will be able to find the motivation that will propel you to make the change that will turn your body around or make you the champion athlete you aspire to be. Here are a few things you can bear in mind to get the champion's mindset:

- Start developing a champion's mindset by winning your mornings. Follow a regular sleeping habit and create a routine that includes exercises, meditation, maybe even a bit of writing, and gratitude.
- Watch talks about agility, resilience, emotional intelligence, leading in crisis, and leadership in times of uncertainty, among other related topics. Many of these may be found for free online.
- If you have a child, ask them what sport they would like to get into, without suggesting any one in particular first. You'll be surprised what sports they will want to do—and just go with it.

My Body Journey

Physically, being in my mid-forties, I can say I am in great shape. I eat well, have no vices, and still maintain the same physicality and strength from when I was an athlete in my teens and twenties. But despite exercising almost every day, I do have high cholesterol, something that seems genetic more than anything. And speaking of genetics, I am most likely a candidate for hypertension at some point. Eight years ago, my mother, at sixty-nine years old, passed away from lymphoma, a type of cancer of the immune system. I feel I did not win the lottery genes-wise, and thus my desire to live as healthy a lifestyle as I can.

Exercise

What I love best about this part of the health equation is your ability to control it. The benefits of compounding cannot be discounted in every aspect of life. I did not get this fit in my mid-forties because I started exercising yesterday, and I am now reaping the benefits of being an athlete since my teens. Since I have never stopped, I have always been fit.

What is important for me is that I make sure to mix things up in terms of the variety and intensity of my exercises. Since the pandemic, I've built a home gym that would allow for me to undergo regular strength training in the comforts of my home. I would do strength training three times a week, making sure I hit all major muscle groups and have a balanced strength training programme.

My all-time favourite piece of equipment is the rowing machine. In a podcast interview on *The Tim Ferris Show*, Hugh Jackman explained that the

155

rowing machine is pretty much the only piece of exercise equipment he needs. If Wolverine sees the benefits of the rower, then I'm all for it. Come to think of it, the rower works out most major muscle groups and is a complete total body workout unto its own.

I use the Technogym Skillrow, which allows me the ability to increase the load through magnetic resistance and gives me the flexibility of either a cardio or strength training power workout. It's a beast and best-in-class since I've always wanted a rower that I would be using for the long haul. I would usually use the rower for a complete body warm up before I engage in my strength training routine.

In between strength training work, I would usually rotate between either a swim, bike, or run/uphill sprints/walk protocol. I always make sure that I have a variety of workouts to make sure that I don't stagnate and get tired of doing the same thing over and over again.

Lately, I have seriously taken up Obstacle Course Racing, specifically Ninja. I knew that this was a new sport that I would seriously get into as, two weeks after recovering from COVID-19, I was able to win the bronze medal in my age group for the Ninja World Cup 100-Metres event held in Manila. It's a relatively new sport and discipline that takes a lot of strength, spatial and kinesthetic intelligence, and mental fortitude. I'm learning new techniques and using all new movements and incorporating them into my workouts. Ah, to be a beginner once again.

Sauna

Another regular routine that I have been into the past years is sauna bathing. Saunas have been widely known to provide a slew of benefits brought about by hormesis or hormetic stress on the body. In essence, hormesis is defined as an adaptive response of cells and organisms to moderate (usually intermittent) stress. Sauna use after working out can help you recover faster and is performance-enhancing. Improved cardiovascular health, flushing of toxins due to sweat production, improved brain health, reduction of stress due to the reduction of cortisol in our blood, and its aid in inducing a deeper sleep at night all make for a strong case for regular sauna use.

Another form of hormetic stress that I will try to start incorporating into my routine is the opposite of the sauna—the cryogenic chamber that I have tried and mentioned in the Brandon Vera Chapter. Until the cost and setup for a cryo chamber goes down to levels where you can have one installed in your home just as you would a sauna, I will have to rely on ice baths in our bathtub for now.

Earlier, I discussed the idea of Longevity Escape Velocity (LEV) and my own attempts to try to achieve even a modicum of this. LEV puts forth the probability that science and medicine can extend your life for more than a year for every year you are alive.

I've since decided to explore the area of functional medicine to at least aid me in this goal. My Functional Medicine Certified Health Coach (FMCHC), Mitch Genato of LifeScience Centre, says they will look at my health in five realms: physiological (biomedical), physical, emotional, mental, and behavioral. Through the process, they will put me through a series of tests to determine everything from my food sensitivities to my predisposition to engaging in certain sports or activities. Mitch shares the functional medicine paradigm and their plans for me:

MG: We can only manage what we can measure and measuring what's going on in your body and understanding how you are biomechanically unique is what will bring you to your optimal self. So, the question I always like to ask people that we engage with is: are you investing in healthcare or waiting to spend for disease? And when companies tell me, 'Oh, we have our HMO,' then, okay, you're waiting to spend on disease. None of it is really about optimizing health and its potential.

The old model was effective when our issue was infectious disease; but now infections are not killing people, but lifestyle diseases are. So, it's just really to paint this picture now when you talk about secondary, tertiary care is disease management, critical care. We're not saying that we should replace that; but what we're saying is there's this imbalance where it's not supported by a strong primary care model of lifestyle management, support groups, and wellness.

So, the twenty-first century medicine, as we frame it, is really the coming together of understanding genomics. When we map the whole human genome, what scientists were able to uncover was that genetics are just 20 per cent of the equation. And the rest of the 80 per cent is really driven by lifestyle and environment. What turns on and off a certain predisposition based on your genetics is your lifestyle. Hence, the outcome is your phenotype, and that's the health that we're measuring. That's why your phenotype is the current snapshot on the current state of your health. So, we know how we can prevent, diagnose, or even treat and reverse disease. That's the relevance of why we're looking at genetics in a clinical setting.

So, what's functional medicine? Basically, it's a methodology. It's a methodical approach to marry what is in the primary care system, which is basically prevention and health optimization, with the disease care paradigm of secondary, tertiary. The lens that we use to look at the signs and the symptoms and the diagnosis is to look at the fundamental organizing systems or core clinical imbalances. And that's driven by antecedents, family medical history, triggers, environmental factors, and mediators, environmental conditions.

We talked about genotype, and we talked about the environment, those are your modifiable lifestyle factors. It's how you sleep and relax. It's how you exercise or move. It's the food you eat. It's how you handle the stress and it's the relationships. So, this is the main scaffolding and framework to our approach.

Basically, the phenotype is an outcome of genomics and the environment having an interplay. So, our intervention focuses on changing your environment because that is how we change the trajectory of your disease potential, which is basically something that we get to see in your genomic profile. So, the benefit of functional medicine is that we're predictive. We're proactive, preventive, and we're participative. In our paradigm, you take the lead. You tell the doctor, you tell our team, what you want. It's your lifestyle that we will have to depend on.

Genetics loads the gun and lifestyle pulls the trigger. So, before we make decisions in terms of why we want to modify our lifestyle, is to always remind ourselves that that's the very stimulus that basically changes the whole conversation on our health.

The Tests

Because eating food is the most common activity that we undertake which drives our health, the first thing Mitch had me undergo was a food intolerance or Food Sensitivity Test (FST). According to the literature for the test, the FST helps you plan for a diet change. It recommends the foods to be eliminated, reduced or rotated, and will provide ideas for alternative or substitute foods. Understanding how to re-introduce foods once symptoms have subsided, will ensure that a varied and balanced diet is adopted, which is essential to maintain good health.

Reactions that trigger an immune response are mostly referred to as 'allergies' and occur when the body overreacts to foods that do not usually produce a response in the majority of people. While the FST is not an allergy test, the folks at LifeScience Centre find that it is a very useful tool in optimizing a person's meal plan that would prioritize absorption of nutrients and mitigation of inflammation.

Since we pretty much eat the same food on a daily basis, my wife Monica and I took the test together. This would help us plan for what foods to avoid and also plan for alternatives.

The results were not encouraging as we were shown the chart that indicates what foods we should avoid. It was quite a long list. Our nutritionist-dietician Jason Villanueva patiently took us through each and every food item.

I am apparently reacting to soy, which I always have every morning when I have soy milk with my cereal, rice, which I eat in almost every meal, potatoes, corn, and oysters. Apart from the malt, which is found in most chocolates, beer and whiskey, I was told I should also avoid. I can do without the beer and whiskey, I'm not sure how I feel about the chocolates. Casein, which is found in whey protein, should also be avoided.

The silver lining is that Jason was able to present alternatives. I could go with quinoa or adlai instead of rice, coconut/walnut/macadamia milk instead of soy or cow's milk, sweet potatoes and cassava instead of potatoes, and for the chocolates, as long as they are 70 per cent dark chocolate, I'm good. He also recommended for me to go as gluten-free as possible, since gluten is pro-inflammatory.

The objective is to be able to have my system take a break from these foods that could be causing my digestive system to be compromised. Each of the food items I would need to avoid would be monitored over twenty-one day cycles to ensure that the IgG load is brought down to a level which leads to optimized absorption of nutrients in my gut.[10]

What we're shooting for as well, in terms of diet intervention, is the diversity of what I eat. A healthy diet is to really have a variety of foods. The more diverse the better. Whole foods, not processed.

An interesting suggestion is how much water intake we should have in a day, to which he calculated based on a rule of thumb: get half your weight in pounds, and multiply by 29.5. That's how many millilitres of water you should be consuming, plus an additional 1 litre for every hour of exercise. Rounding up my numbers, I should consume at least 3 litres of water per day.

Apart from the FST, I also underwent other tests that had me give blood, urine, and DNA swab samples for. These were sent to labs abroad in the US and Austria to be evaluated and released by genetics counselors and molecular biologists.

---

[10] IgG Immunoglobin G is the most common antibody. It's in blood and other body fluids, and protects against bacterial and viral infections.

The first is a Micronutrient Sensor, which can help identify weaknesses in the metabolism. It examines your micronutrients, amino acids, proteins, other metabolism components, detoxification, and microbiome health.

The next is a Performance Sensor, which analyses my athletic genes and my genetic predispositions to being either a power or endurance athlete, my Maximal Oxygen Uptake (VO2 Max) or my genetic capability to absorb oxygen through the lungs and transport it to the appropriate muscles, my inflammatory responses and analysis of my risk of injury, my optimal performance nutrition, and a food list assessed according to my genes to help me plan my nutrition optimally.

The last is a genetic panel called a Premium Sensor Plus, which measures how our genes influence our health and will give me a snapshot of my physiological predisposition. This will map everything from how my body breaks down and cleans out the drugs in my body to understanding my predisposition to disease conditions such as cancer (because of what my mom went through), cardiovascular health risks (including hypertension), neurological conditions, metabolic risks or how my body will age by looking into my bones, joints, eye and teeth health as well as my hormones as I enter 'male menopause' or andropause age.

With preventive tips included in my Gene Panel, it is designed not to strike fear based on my disease risks but, instead, to empower me to understand what lifestyle factors could drive my genes to be turned 'on' or 'off' based on my epigenetics. The caution, according to Mitch, is also that I don't take the results as Bible truth but to essentially validate my results individually with the help of the medical team in LifeScience.

My results were both predictable and surprising:

MG: What is phenomenal is the uptake of your body of nutrients. You're blessed with good genes. I guess that's where your inclination or predisposition to being very athletic comes from. Your body responds well to physical conditioning.

In terms of you wanting to optimize performance further, we know specific areas where you need that last mile or extra mile. To begin with for your VO2 Max, your oxygen uptake is not ideal. You're below average. Which doesn't mean you don't perform well. That's where your training and conditioning pays off.

The muscle profile you have is leaning more towards endurance, except your VO2 Max is low. Which means if you want to excel more in your endurance sports, that's where high altitude training, hyperbaric oxygen therapy, and breathing techniques come into play.

Your micronutrients, flying colours.

The Gene test is a reference to bump against what you're feeling and what is real to you right now. This tells us what you're designed for but how you live your life affects how that design is manifesting.

For example, based on the results there is a recommendation for you to increase your uptake of antioxidants such as Vitamin A, C, and E, and N-Acetyl Cysteine (NAC). Berries, fruits have natural antioxidants as well. When you know that your workload will increase, that's when you help yourself by increasing your antioxidants.

Your amino acid levels are fantastic already. Your Valine and Arginine are less than ideal levels. Pumpkin seeds are a good source of Valine and Arginine. White meat such as turkey, pork loin and chicken are good sources of arginine, as are spirulina, chickpeas and lentils. For Valine, tuna, oatmeal (steel cut as opposed to instant).

Another piece of good news, because of your genes, even your ability to detox from chemicals, air pollutants, is quite optimal.

These pretty much sum up your metabolic profile and micronutrient sensor. It goes to show that you're living a healthy lifestyle. It becomes more interesting if you want to maximize your genetic panel if you will be participating in an event. There's specific pre-season, during season and postseason recommendations on your food intake. We can bring in your nutritionist to really fine-tune that.

The one we can spend more time on and really digging deeper in is your Premium Plus Sensor, which talks about the inevitable which is the ageing part. I even looked at your oncology risk. You don't seem to share the same genetic risk for cancer as your mother. Cross referencing that to your lifestyle and nutrient levels, it's showing very promising results. Whatever you've been investing in over these last four decades is paying off. We can even say you're like the poster child for a healthy lifestyle.

Moving forward, what we would need to monitor would be if there are any remarkable changes. Something that we recognize from a lifestyle perspective is that, as we succeed in life, there are more things to watch out for such as vices, sleep deprivation, and the demands of our lifestyle changes. The nature of your job, as much as we love traveling, traveling is one of the biggest contributors to oxidative stress. Just being in an airplane is a lot of oxidative stress. The recycled air, and how travel sometimes disrupts sleep and routine.

The fact that your VO2 Max is not optimal can explain why you're more comfortable in power sports. It is a sort of a handicap, not to say that you are defined by it. But it just means it will take extra effort for you to optimize your endurance performance. In your profile, in terms of power and endurance, you're in the middle. But in terms of muscle fiber, you're extreme on the endurance side.

JA: This, I find, is highly surprising. I've always thought I had more fast twitch muscles than slow twitch as I was a sprinter and power athlete back in the day.

MG: But because of your condition training, you're able to optimize the power side and work with a handicap of VO2 Max not being as optimal. But if you really want to optimize the prowess of your muscle design, there's a lot of promise in endurance if you can support your VO2 Max. Since you're on the extreme end of the endurance metre, and if you're doing well in power sports, it only goes to show how superior your conditioning training has been. Your genes are very athletic by design.

JA: On a final note, what this tells me is that our genes do not really define what our bodies can do. As a young athlete, I've always believed I was made more for power sports and short bursts of speed, so I trained for power and eventually became the fastest junior sprinter at the time. Had I known I was made more for endurance, would I have switched to perhaps doing the marathon instead? I highly doubt it. Part of the reason why I loved the 100-metre dash is that I wanted to be the fastest man of the games. It was my dream, and I wouldn't stop until I achieved it.

This reminds me of the 1997 movie *Gattaca*, which paints a picture of a not-so-distant dystopian world where genetically engineered humans are produced by genetically enhanced human reproduction. Children born the 'natural' way were discriminated against by their genetically superior counterparts, who were optimal in every way and had tremendous advantages in securing higher level jobs. The protagonist Vincent, who was born of 'natural' means, was able to fulfill his dream of becoming an astronaut by impersonating a genetically superior, Jerome, a man who was disfigured in a debilitating accident and sold his identity to Vincent. Vincent 'faked it till he made it' and managed to secure a mission to a moon in Saturn.

Stealing Jerome's identity did not change Vincent's capabilities. He was always capable of performing well in his field, but his genes as his society would want to dictate would never have given him the chance to prove that he can be better than most. One of my favourite scenes showed him performing a monitored run on a treadmill. He manipulated the sensor to make it seem like his heart was handling the stress levels well and, when he was out of the room, we see him gasping for air as his real heart rate was, in fact, racing uncontrollably. He just couldn't show it. The most impressive thing about the movie is how a 'genetically inferior' Vincent was able to perform at such a high level against his genetically superior counterparts because, despite his limitations, he worked hard and smart to make the grade.

How do I explain my successes as a sprinter during my younger years? A 100 per cent mindset. I wanted it, I worked hard, and despite my muscles being made for endurance, I was able to make my body perform as a top sprinter. The body follows what the mind—and our heart—desires. Only now, after discovering what my body is really made for, do I see and appreciate how much of a feat this really was.

Act 2: Body Key Takeaways

What are my key takeaways for this section on the body? *Mens sana in corpore sano* is a latin phrase I've kept as a mantra from my alma mater Ateneo de Manila University, translated as 'A sound mind in a sound body.' This rings true for almost all of my interviews for this section as the mind has always had a symbiotic relationship with the body that makes the optimal function of one almost always dependent on the other. Mindset is almost always key to a sound body. My favourite takeaways will help you develop the right mindset when thinking of your body:

'The best way is to educate yourself on the right kind of diet, and to keep yourself active. Weight loss shouldn't be the main goal. You won't be able to sustain it if your only purpose is to lose weight, because then it won't stick. It's not going to become a lifestyle. We're not after perfection, but progress.'

—Pia Wurtzbach

'And now that I'm older, now that I'm wise to the world, I see how things move. I understand. Mother Nature can't kick our ass. People can't kick our ass, me losing our title from our last event doesn't sadden me as much. I'm going to come get that thing back. We just get over things. We make things happen.'

—Brandon Vera

'I love sports and I saw how it helped me. By playing team sports, it taught me so many values that I consider to be indispensable in life. Focus, hard work, determination, discipline, teamwork are just some of the things that I think sports teaches. I think it's been helpful for me all the way through my career to my adult life. I really honestly believe that every kid growing up should have a chance to play sports so that they can learn all these values.'

—Toby Claudio

'I think the way I've approached the game is just different now. The way the injury taught me that, you know, in the snap of a finger, my career could be over. Therefore, today might be the last day that I'm doing this. I'm going to give it my all, that's something that I always say and it's written on my door every single day. That is just me. That's maybe the difference in the way I approach my sport.'

—Ernest John 'EJ' Obiena

'Out of all the sports that I've done and participated in, Spartan is the most fulfilling. It combines a lot of different tasks and body movements and skill sets. It's the greatest parallel to life, where if you don't train hard enough for something you won't be successful in it. You can get by; you can cross the finish line, but if you want to cross the finish line a champ you've got to work for it.'

—Rovilson Fernandez

'Don't always to be so fast-paced. Learn to let go . . . There's a Chinese saying that if you were to grab a handful of sand, the tighter you grip the sand, the more sand will leak out from your fingers. So, I think that concept is very similar . . . You must learn to let go sometimes to relax.'

—Chien Han How

'Especially at my age, I tell people, who cannot do a 5, 10, 15-minute walk? I posted a story about a classmate. We talked about his exercise regimen, everything that he needs to get him out of his wheelchair because he just had his lower legs amputated. I'm saying here is a guy who has no legs and he's concerned about his physical fitness regimen, so what's your excuse?'

—Chot Reyes

In the next, concluding section on the soul, we go to the most esoteric aspect of people's lives, as we go on a deep exploration of our spiritual, higher self.

Act 3: Soul

'The things you think about determine the quality of your mind. Your soul takes on the colour of your thoughts.'

—Marcus Aurelius

For this concluding section on the soul, I've interviewed people who have transcended to the uppermost level of Maslow's hierarchy of needs and give the world the ways by which they are able to self-actualize beyond the usual preoccupations of the mind and body.

International recording artist Anggun shares her passion for music and embracing her authenticity while having the perspective of not taking her being a celebrity and what she does too seriously.

Award-winning poet and author Bryan Thao Worra likewise infuses a great sense of patriotism to his body of work, and encourages the youth, the 'radical, liberating feeling to dare to speak amid the storm and waves'.

Serial entrepreneur and biotechnology investor Gautam Godhwani puts his money where his mouth is by backing alternative meat technologies that impact the world and really move the needle in terms of food sustainability.

Bangladeshi fashion icon and former international model Bibi Russell uses her experience, influence, and heritage to make a powerful statement and sustainable livelihood for countless craftspeople, elevating their lives, and the way we see fashion, in the process.

Last, the Art of Living Foundation's Nameeta Dargani takes us through a journey inwards with breathing and meditation techniques, and helps us explore the Self, the ultimate level of our existence.

Anggun

International multilingual recording artist and music icon

'Try to do good every day to others just because.'

Embrace your authenticity

Anggun took the world by storm when she launched her international singing career with the release of the song 'Snow on the Sahara'. Her voice captivated music fans; a fresh smooth sound that soothes the soul.

Her path to international stardom wasn't as smooth as it is for Asian performers today. Coming from a successful career as a rock singer in Indonesia, Anggun made a huge leap of going pop with a hint of jazz. In early 1994, she went to Europe. Three years later, she found herself in France launching one of the best-selling albums ever by an Asian artist.

Today, Anggun lives in her adopted country, France, with her husband and daughter. Still singing and performing, Anggun is a judge on the television series, Masked Singer. Previously, she was one of the judges of Asia's Got Talent and a mentor in the Indonesian versions of Got Talent and The Voice.

Always proud of her heritage, Anggun continues to be an inspiration for Asians, especially in a region often overlooked (southeast Asia) because of its small size, who want to make it big in the worldwide stage.

On music

In Indonesia, music is not really considered as something very serious. Up until today, I still think that what I do is not really important compared to teachers or compared to doctors. What I do is to entertain people and I always feel that I'm just here to entertain. There's nothing serious about it. It's about music, but I try to do it wholeheartedly and I try to put meanings into my songwriting because again, it's just music.

I don't think music can change the world. It can change your perception of the world, but it's not a tool; it's not something so powerful. Music is my life, but there's some kind of a blurry line between what my personal life is and what music is. There is always like a soundtrack playing in my head, whatever it is I'm doing, and so it is important. But how I feel . . . like a lot of musicians nowadays think too much of themselves and it's becoming bigger than who they are. I think, at the end of the day, you just have to enjoy it. It's just music. It's to share with people. I always tell new singers, 'Enjoy it. It's just music. You have to have that love and passion, but that's it.' You have to be serious about it and you have to put your skills in, you have to put all the goodness, all the positive energy and everything you want to put into your music. But that's it, don't get it bigger than your head. Don't believe in your own promotion. It's just everything now it's all so blurry. That's what I meant by it.

On authenticity

I really believe that honesty has to be upfront. It's really hard, but I try to be who I am as a person as an artist. I would never wish to conceal who I am as a person. I come from Indonesia, I'm a proud Javanese woman and I speak with my accent. I'm not trying to absorb somebody else's culture and/or accent. I think individuality is very important nowadays, especially in the world where everyone sounds a bit the same on the radio. You have to find your strong points and identity. Having that identity is very important, and keeping it is very important as well. This is actually what differentiates you from all the others and it is hard because I did not have role models. When I started my career internationally, that is one of the most important things: to keep my identity, to keep who I am as an artist, as a person, and as a woman.

On being proud of your heritage

My fourteen-year-old daughter speaks Indonesian, French, and English fluently. The fact that she speaks Indonesian is one of my greatest joys and pride because I am the only Indonesian pillar that she has here. I speak Indonesian even to animals. I see dogs on the street. I would just talk to them in Indonesian. It's not an effort for me but it's an effort for her because she goes to school, then she has to converse with me in Indonesian. But for me, it is super important because whenever I come back to Indonesia or to Jakarta, I see that even my friends speak English to their kids. They put their kids to international schools—which is fine because my father used to put me into Catholic school and we're Muslims so it's just to have a different kind of opinion—but then they keep the language at home as well, then sometimes the kids their kids don't speak Indonesian any more. They only speak English to their nannies. It doesn't make sense to me. You have to be proud of your own language. It makes you richer culturally. You have to always keep that. My daughter eats rice and cheese, speaks Indonesian, French, and English and, yes, I believe those will be useful tools for her later on.

On the things she loves doing

The secret before any concerts? I don't know. I would prepare my voice by resting. I sing daily, for myself, for probably half an hour. I don't actually work out, which is bad. I don't like to sweat, and this is something that I will try to rectify because I want to be able to have more energy. But I'm not a gym buff. I have to do certain things my own way, in my own time, like pilates.

I love to eat. I love food. Being in France, my husband cooks divinely well. I also love to drink. I love everything that life can give me but in moderation, of course, because I don't believe in depriving yourself of all the goodness.

I believe that a woman should age gracefully. If you think you need to have a certain help cosmetically, then go ahead. I have never done any procedures. I believe that as Asians we're kind of blessed.

On fame and wealth

People want to be famous but being famous can be a burden if they don't know what they are not famous for. They think that a lot of things are going to be easier once you're famous, but it's not. Or people want to be rich; they think that it solves all the problems but it's not. Rich people do have problems as well and their problems are probably even bigger than yours and mine. I welcome everything; I welcome wholeheartedly everything that is thrown my way, and I try to be graceful whenever hard times arrive. I try to be humble whenever I'm riding a good wave. Life is made of that—ups and downs—and you have to want to be down if you want to go up.

On learning new things

Try to surprise yourself. Go and try to live abroad. Talk to everyone. Have friends from different walks of life or from different ages. Be friends with your neighbours and go backpacking around the world and try to learn about the world. Try to see how other people live and you might learn a thing or two about not only the world but about yourself, and about your ability to adapt yourself. Try to fast. Muslims do fasting during Ramadan but try to do that just within your own term; it could be three days or it could be a week. Try that and try to test not only your physical ability but your mental ability. Read biographies of great people of the world. Read the biography of Mahatma Gandhi or the Dalai Lama or Steve Jobs. Try to do good every day to others just because. Live completely free and give yourself a good gift once a year.

Fast Talk with John

What makes you Indonesian?

Whenever I see myself in the mirror, I see my parents, my hair, I hear my accent, I see my heritage. My name is also what makes me Indonesian. I will never ever change anything about who I am. I don't have to wear a *batik* or Indonesian fabric to make people believe I'm from Indonesia. I don't need that; I am Indonesian and it's in my blood.

Is there anything from your country that you would like the world to know about or discover?

If you go to Indonesia, you know that it's all about cultural heritage; it's about centuries and centuries of traditions and stories and legends and mythology and everything when you go there and you see it, you see some kind of examples of it you feel like it's true there are certain things that cannot be told you just have to be there and see it and breathe it.
Visit:

- **Yogyakarta**, which is the centre of Java
- **Borobudur**, which is the oldest Buddhist temple in the world. It's from the ninth century and so majestic that it would take your breath away. Wake up around 4 a.m. and walk up the stairs. There are carvings made out of volcanic stones. The seventh level doesn't have one because it means the absence of everything.
- **Bali** and go to the rice fields. There's something very different and very super calming about being surrounded by rice fields.
- **Tanatorraja** in Sulawesi, I went there when I was about thirteen.

If you could give a commencement speech (if you haven't already), what message would you want to impart?

We, as people, have the huge capacity to adapt ourselves and this is where we can actually try out something or test ourselves into something. Young people have the time, the will, and the energy to do and to conquer the world. Anything is still very possible; you just have to work hard on it and be willing to fail. Be willing to make mistakes because it's from the mistakes that you're going to learn. We have to give more time to the younger generation. We have to be more gentle to them. This whole cancel culture is dangerous. I think we have to be able to make mistakes. We have to be able to learn from it and be more loving. If we do not show that to the younger generation, they will never be able to perpetuate that. So, my message to them is that go ahead; go, do something, no matter what, just do it. Do what you think makes your heart full and make yourself proud. If you fail, just do it again, try again, try again and learn. It will only make you bolder, stronger, and smarter.

What would your epitaph say?

I never thought of that. I have never actually given that a thought. I would say that I have loved, and I have been loved and blessed and thankful for the ride. I'm blessed. I know that I'm blessed, yes.

If there is anything specific you do that you would recommend I try, what would it be?

You have to say good things, read good books, and see the world.

I would stop watching TV hours before going to bed because I don't want to burden myself with all the negativities in the world. We already have enough problems.

I would recommend to have a lot of sex.

My Thoughts

It is quite refreshing to hear Anggun, a multi-lingual, multi-awarded international recording artist speak about not taking herself and her music too seriously. Quite often we are inundated by the noise of people who seem to be on constant self-promotion and hype. To hear her say that 'it's just music' is the hallmark of a true artist. I guess you can say that music is her profession, but it is, at its core, an expression of her being.

On the authenticity front, embracing your heritage, particularly in this day and age where social media tends to lead a lot of people into a herd or groupthink mentality, having a strong connection to your uniqueness and culture is definitely a strong suit one must take full advantage and ownership of.

Anggun has seen the dangers of cancel culture, and this has probably caused a lot of the younger generation to take fewer risks, to favour the safe side, perhaps to make less mistakes and avoid failure. And this is perhaps the irony of extreme political correctness and the woke generation. We take ourselves too seriously. Yet we must respect our right to be, and the actions we take to express the inequalities and social injustice we find ourselves battling.

Chapter Assignments

Authenticity is a powerful expression of one's soul. Anggun has embraced this fully but, in the same breath, espouses the need to discover new things about the world and how other people live. Some things you may want to discover for yourself or about others:

- Make friends from different walks of life and from different ages. You may not have much in common at first, but it is the differences that might make your friendship a rich tapestry of new possibilities and experiences.
- Travel, see the world on your own. It can be the time for you to know yourself better or find out what you are capable of. Go backpacking, but still take caution by letting people close to you know where you are going. Have a lifeline or emergency contact where people can reach you and vice versa.
- And as you try to see the world, why not also explore your own country and enrich yourself with your heritage. Sometimes you do not have to go very far to experience something new or meet interesting people you otherwise would never have met. Get a map of your country, close your eyes, and go to where your finger lands. Whether alone or with friends or family, this exercise would be good for your soul.

Bryan Thao Worra

Lao-American Author/Poet
President, Science Fiction Poetry Association
Member, Horror Writer Association

**'A single seed can become a forest.
A single heart can transform a nation.'**

My heritage is a strength

Lao-American writer Bryan Thao Worra is a recipient of numerous literature and poetry fellowships. An award-winning poet and author, Worra lifts Asian Americans in the literary world with his advocacy campaigns. His involvement with community service allows him to be in touch constantly with humanity and use his craft to put these causes forward.

Worra wears his heritage like a badge of honour that, instead of being acknowledged as an Asian American author, he prefers to be labeled as Lao-American.

An innate achiever, Worra had to change schools because he was always ahead of his classmates. At an early age, he became aware of the challenges of coming from a different race from where he grew up in. This paved the way for him to grow empathetic towards the plight of others.

He merged this burning empathy with his creative side and the result are works that dig deep through social issues, humanity, passion, and compassion.

On growing up in America as an Asian

My childhood was pretty typical for any child adopted by an American pilot who flew in Laos during the final years of the Central Intelligence Agency's (CIA) Secret War in Laos, and right before the end of the Vietnam War. I became a US citizen during the American Bicentennial at the age of three in Montana, with years spent in Alaska and Michigan before going to college in Ohio, and on to a career in the non-profit field in Washington DC and Minnesota. In 2003, I went back to Laos for the very first time in thirty years and learned that my long-lost family had, in fact, escaped to America and was living in the city of Modesto.

In the early years, my parents quickly found out that public schools weren't a great place for me because the teachers were trying to fail me in class for reading ahead and typically finishing the workbooks in a single hour. So, I found myself in a number of Lutheran private schools and, ultimately, the Rudolf Steiner School of Ann Arbor, where I thrived and found a good match for my creative side and more formal lessons. I discovered, by the second grade, that I had a good head for the social sciences and the humanities, and a passion for language and the different types of stories people told around the globe.

In Michigan, one of the important formative incidents for me as a child was the 1982 slaying of a Chinese American man, Vincent Chin. He was killed in Detroit by two former auto workers who thought they'd been laid off because of the Japanese. As a Lao child, I came to understand that I'd often be mistaken for other races and cultures as well, and I developed a sense of empathy that led me to advocate for justice for everyone and to recognize the challenges of navigating race and culture as an adoptee.

But in the arts, I had an ability to express myself and navigate those feelings and interests in a way that many other refugees and immigrants from Laos did not in the early years of our diaspora.

On overcoming his own challenges

There weren't many people who had ever heard of Laos, the country I was born in, and there were few books or articles I could turn to learn about my heritage. But people don't just come out of nowhere, and it's important to have a sense of that in order to understand not only who we've been, but who we might become. Because this was the first decade since the end of the Vietnam War, and there was a lot of anti-Japanese sentiment because many US auto workers hated the overseas competition, I often got mistaken for 'the enemy', even as many of my fellow refugees, immigrants, and I arrived in the US because we'd been allies during the southeast Asian conflicts.

Overcoming the ignorance of others while also charting my own sense of my possibilities were the challenges that stick out most in my mind from those days.

On becoming a writer

That's now a long time ago and I've come to a way of thinking that understands a writer, especially a poet, has a thousand beginnings, really. There's the first time they see a book. The first time they run into a poem. The first time they try, and the first time they make a poem they think they're happy with. There's the first time they meet a person they want to write a poem for. There's a moment their poem is criticized for the first time and gets meaningful feedback or validation. There's a moment when poetry becomes easy for them, and one where poetry is difficult, and they decide to keep pushing through, anyway. Which of these is *the* moment?

For me, I often think about the first poem I wrote that wasn't a class assignment. Like many poets, I had written it for someone I was attracted to. In my case, it somehow wound up being a poem involving Batman, masks, the opera *Pagliacci*, and some other things. I didn't even get a date with the girl, but I did end up with a nice poem instead, and that turned out to be for the best, anyway. Alas, I lost the poem years ago. That sort of thing happens. But I kept going anyway to see what else I could write.

On writing

I know there are some people who operate with strict routines and a methodical, almost scientific process. Mine takes more of its cues from the idea of MBWA: Management By Wandering Around. You need discipline to not get scatter-brained or wholly random in this process. But the ideal to me is to be nimble and to see constant connections between everything and write on what others tend not to focus on.

I typically identify the bigger theme I ultimately hope I and my reader can walk away with. From there, I consider a few other principles and ideas that can be connected to that. I imagine the most obvious approach and then say. 'That's boring,' and search for a different way to express it that might stick in someone's memory. Often, this entails non-intuitive pruning and searching for ways to embed 'easter eggs' into the text that can reward a reader.

I don't take particular joy in my work sounding like another person's contributions to a given project. Especially in my own books, I feel that while there can be interconnections between pieces, I think each poem or story should be in there for a specific and surprising reason, with very few redundancies. Or what's the point?

On discipline

I often think about Mark Twain's quip, 'I never let school stand in the way of a good education.' I grew up with a distinct mix of teachers: Some were subtly or overtly racist and unsupportive, especially in Alaska. But in Michigan, I was fortunate to have those who encouraged me constantly to go beyond the assigned, and to give in to my innate curiosity. The trick was to find a way to be disciplined in my search, but open to outcomes, not attached to outcomes.

Several of my high school teachers encouraged me to embrace the ideal of the 'renaissance man' and ideas of cultural literacy, which has since fallen out of vogue, but it was important for me growing up to get into a mindset that I could study and seek out knowledge across a wide range of interests and disciplines.

Years later, I ran into a fellow southeast Asian writer who was somewhat mystified when it became clear that, when I went to college, I was genuinely just trying to learn things, not getting onto some career track or a professional credential or make a networking contact that would be key to some entrepreneurial venture decades from now.

On awards and fellowships

I'm grateful for all of the awards and distinctions I've received over the years, and it's difficult to single any one of them out. But I think we'll all agree that being selected as a Cultural Olympian representing the nation of Laos during the London Summer Games of 2012 is understandably memorable.

Receiving the United States National Endowment for the Arts Fellowship in Literature for poetry in 2009 was an important milestone for me. In the fifty-five years since the Fellowship was first established, out of over 3,400 recipients, I remain the only Lao poet to receive this distinction since our diaspora began. As someone who didn't major in English and didn't receive an MFA, this was a significant accomplishment.

Ten years later, I received a 2019 Joyce Award with the Lao Assistance Centre that provided us $50,000 for me to create a groundbreaking exhibit of poetry and art responding to forty-five years of Lao refugees in America—but before we could show it the way we planned, the world was plunged into a global pandemic. I'll never forget that.

On growing community service

All of our stories are intertwined with one another. As the old proverb goes, 'wars begin when we stop caring about other people's children'. Many people sacrificed greatly to move our societies forward to something stable and prosperous, and it is important for us to see ourselves as part of the great chain of being. It's a joy to ease the way for others. In times I had few resources to help myself, I could still help others, and that gave me the motivation to keep going.

You'll find that in life, when helping others, more doors always open than close.

On helping southeast Asian writers

As we've seen time and time again, often the most important ideas that change the world can come from the most unexpected places. Gregor Mendel discovered the principles of heredity as a monk in a remote Russian monastery. George Lucas began in the Central Valley of California and went on to create Star Wars. The theory of evolution began with a visit to the Galapagos Islands.

This isn't to say southeast Asian writers are guaranteed to put forward a galaxy-changing idea in the near future, but if we don't encourage them, what might we lose?

On heritage

Absolutely. I didn't see my heritage as a liability, but a strength, especially since in the US, for nearly fifty years, there were fewer than fifty books by

Lao writers in our own words, on our own terms while rebuilding our lives here in the aftermath of the Vietnam War and the Secret War. It's important to understand that my approach wasn't centred on repeating what had already been said, but on challenging our assumptions, looking for the best of our journey to celebrate, and to examine the moments when we could have done better and to find the untold stories we need to hear.

Over the years, I've found my approach often resonated with many outside of the Lao community, because they saw how important it was for their people to also have a similar approach to their traditions, their heritage, and their future.

On his influences

My grandmother arguably played the biggest role in setting me on the writer's path. I treasure memories of her letting me read to my heart's content while exposed to a global mix of art and culture at museums and TV, from the BBC to PBS, old US sitcoms and science fiction. She let me watch the pop culture of the time, but she insisted I also see *everything*. Highbrow, lowbrow, the mediocre and the sublime. There were gems in everything, and there were some real clunkers. But it was always okay to look for the best that really moved me.

Outside of my family, I often credit the Asian American creator, Larry Hama. He wrote an eighties comic book series called *G.I. Joe* as an assignment literally no one else at the company wanted to take. They thought it was a career killer. But he went above and beyond to create a story filled with humour and social critique, rich characters, and challenging motivations month in, month out, and never took the lazy way out to approach the task. More significantly, in a time when you couldn't always centre an Asian American experience directly in the comics, he still managed to address this in his own way.

Among poets, I can point to three poems in particular that cemented my journey, Heather McHugh's 'What He Said', Pablo Neruda's 'Y Cuanto Vive (And How Long?)', and Yevgeny Yevtushenko's 'People'. But I'll let readers look at these themselves to see what they might get out of it.

On literature and the youth

Literature's role in any society is not static, but dynamic. Sometimes it leads to dangerous ends. If people engage with literature poorly, it can lead to tremendous injustice, disparities, even potential genocides. But the opposite is also possible, and a good literary tradition continues to connect people at an individual level to greater national and international conversations on the human experience across centuries.

Literature helps us to see what our elders and ancestors were reaching for, what they dreamed of, and how we've changed and grown. Good literature anchors us to existence even amid uncertainties and turmoil, reassuring us that we're often not the very first people to confront particular calamities. If we read more consistently and took lessons to heart from literature, we might well have avoided numerous problems today. Sometimes we need to affirm ideas found in older books, and sometimes we need to challenge those ideas and present something better even though we know, someday, our own descendants will likely roll their eyes at our best ideas for our time.

We're constantly creating content these days with such little appreciation for what truly lasts. What things might be said that are worth giving permanence to, to commit to the form of a book and to pass on to future generations. As writers, there's a deep thrill that's hard to explain even after centuries. But for our youth, it's a radical, liberating feeling to dare to speak amid the storm and waves, to find a constant notion, an idea that is so badly needed in the world that, centuries later, people might return to because you've reshaped the way we envision solving a particular problem or circumstance. Not everything you write will meet these criteria, but it's infinitely rewarding when you find the words that do.

On Laos history oversight

I'm currently working on a number of new books including a historical timeline that expands our understanding of the Lao diaspora in the United States from 1975 to the present. In nearly fifty years in the US, among over twenty-nine major timelines of the US and Asian American history, the Lao experience has been almost completely excluded. So, if no one else is going to bother correcting that oversight, I felt compelled to take that project on.

Fast Talk with John:

What makes you Asian?

That's a question that can quickly get philosophical in 10,000 ways, but beyond a question of genetics, the customs and traditions I observe within my daily practice are often in response to something with ties to an Asian mindset, history, or imagination. Naturally, my passion and interest can ebb depending on other circumstances going on in the world. But it is in the Asian experience where I consistently find my sense of myself returning to when I need to find my centre.

Is there anything from Laos (food, place, custom) that you would like the world to know about or discover?

Laos is a very old country with over 700 plus years of tradition. Surrounded by so many nations and cultures in that time, including an era under French Indochina and our relationship with the US in the twentieth century, as Lao, we had ample opportunity to give up those customs and traditions but did not. Even those living in diaspora beyond the historical borders of Laos today continue to pass on our traditions, language, and ideals.

Entire books remain to be written about what those are and why they mean so much to us but at the centre of much of our journey is a desire for harmony, inclusion, compassion, and the search for wisdom even in crisis.

Who, to you, is a modern-day superhero? What special power does this hero possess?

Most mothers are of course the modern-day superheroes anywhere in the globe; juggling so many things often beyond the sight and notice of their children and families, sacrificing much to give others a chance, a reason for hope.

I know who I'd personally consider a modern-day superhero, but I'm pledged to keep their identity a secret so that they can keep doing the amazing work they do in the world the way they need to. But I will say their superpowers include patience, generosity, and tremendous artistic talent even as they are far too often unsung out there. You know who you are.

If you could give a commencement speech (if you haven't already), what message would you want to impart?

There are many messages I try to impart in any given year, but among those, I tend to share lately: teach yourself the skills to imagine a future you can see yourself in. Passionately engage with that imagination to understand the many possibilities before you, and how to act upon them in a way that brings the greatest benefit not just to yourself, but to others.

Be helpful, and actively seek ways to improve the quality of life for those around you. When you go into the world with that mindset, rather than focusing solely on your own advancement and enrichment, you will find a great many more doors will open.

Something I've found deeply important for students to hear is that even though their families and community might not always express it in the way we might see others saying this to their children, it remains true: 'We love you. Keep going. Keep dreaming. Remember.'

What keeps you up at night? What gets you up in the morning?

Our lives are finite, and I don't take the time I have in the cosmos for granted. In my culture, there are still subjects our community has not written about or responded to. While I cannot 'write all of the things', I often consider what would not show up in our body of literature and art for a long time if I didn't write them.

A great and gnawing sense of curiosity gets me up each morning, but I smile with a particular joy at this because I chose a path where I don't dread meeting quotas or filing reports, but instead have to exercise a particularly high level of liberty to explore and create, knowing that every project I complete is helping to rebuild and expand my culture and our shared heritage that was nearly destroyed during the wars of the twentieth century.

How do you prepare for what you do? Any special routines you can share?

Often my preparation as a poet involves a mix of photography, sketching, painting, scribbling, and rough drafts on scrap papers before I start typing the final desired poem on a computer. In this process, I feel I gain useful prototypes from this. Looking at the photos and other artworks, and then looking at my poem, if I've done it well, it will be clear why the poem had to be a poem and not something else.

But probably the most important routine I would encourage others to incorporate into their lives is to learn how to study and create in different spaces and under different time limits as best you can.

When we spend too much time studying and creating in one, and only one, space at a set hour and time, when an examination or presentation comes up, many often blank out because they only know the material or technique in the comfort of their homes or a particular library desk or coffee shop. As a poet, you have to learn to be prepared for any number of intrusions and unexpected circumstances throwing off performance or discussion. Training for uncertainty can save you a lot of grief.

What do you do in your downtime? How do you regain focus?

I tend to travel and look for things to study that others wouldn't expect me to study and seek out. I particularly enjoy learning about the histories and ideas that don't always get included in the books.

I don't think focus has ever been a big challenge for me because I anchored so much of my process to history, understanding where I and my various projects and interests stood in relation to things such as the fiftieth anniversary of our diaspora or key opportunities and moments coming up between 5–100 years from now.

In rare moments where I was 'adrift', I found a big solution was to cut out toxic people in my life or to at least understand them as they truly were and to revise my relationships to them meaningfully.

What is the one thing you wish you could have known or learned sooner?

How to accept help from others. It's still not something I'm great at, but I'm growing within that question.

What would your epitaph say?

'A single seed can become a forest. A single heart can transform a nation.'

If there is anything specific (or unique) you do that you would recommend people try, what would it be?

People often spend a great deal of time trying to improve themselves, to gain the skills to succeed as leaders and community builders. But I believe it is just as important to learn how to fail and risk like a leader, especially for those with refugee and immigrant roots.

When success occurs, there's no shortage of people who want to be around you to share in your victory. But the people you truly want in your life are the ones who stand by you even in failure; who come back to the table and ask what you will do next to try again, time and time again. Those are the most interesting people you need to keep an eye out for.

My Thoughts

Bryan is clearly a nationalist, wearing his country's flag on his sleeve as much as he does his passion for writing. I share this nationalism for my own country, the Philippines, with its beauty and potential clearly depicted in my TV shows, and in this book.

I believe people like Bryan and I have a responsibility to make our voices heard, in whatever shape or form that would reach those who need to hear our message. Are there less and less people reading books? I would think so if we compare it to decades past pre-internet. But books will always be written and there will always be people who would seek the deep connection of the written—and not the tweeted—word.

Bryan says that 'Good literature anchors us to existence even amid uncertainties and turmoil, reassuring us that we're often not the very first people to confront particular calamities.' Despite my attempts for it to be evergreen, the snapshot in time when the interviews were conducted and when this book was written, still reeling from the COVID pandemic and its effects on the world, reflect the sentiments of our time. And perhaps that's not an entirely bad thing. We can all take a page from other people's experiences, and this particular one in our history is one that, perhaps, can serve to reassure a future troubled soul searching for answers.

Chapter Assignments

How nationalistic are you? You may not express your heritage to the lengths Bryan does for Laos, but there are many ways you can show your love for your country:

- When was the last time you read a book about your country or heritage that was not required reading in school? Try to sink your teeth into one that clearly aims to stoke national pride or ignite a deep sense and understanding of your heritage.
- For your next trip abroad, buy a lapel pin of your country's flag, and wear it in a social function or business event that you go to. You can literally wear your country's flag on your sleeve to show your pride and love of country.
- Find an advocacy in your country that will empower the marginalized. Find a way to help them become the best versions of themselves. Sometimes, a person just needs a break to break free.

Gautam Godhwani

Managing Partner, Good Startup
Serial Entrepreneur and Investor

**'You can almost measure your life by the degree of continuity
that you have in areas that matter to you.'**

Technology as a catalyst for innovation and sustainability

Gautam Godhwani grew up in Silicon Valley, working at International Business Machines Corp. (IBM), Hewlett-Packard Company (HP), and Microsoft, learning not only about technology but also about business operations. After years of starting and exiting two technology-centric startups (Simply Hired and AtWeb), he started investing in companies focused on providing sustainable choices to consumers.

186

He moved to Singapore to help fund research and development of startups that utilize biotechnology to come up with the best meat alternatives. Godhwani raised $40,000,000 in funding for the non-governmental organization (NGO) he co-founded, the India Community Centre, which has several facilities in the San Francisco Bay Area. Godhwani believes that for people to make a conscious effort in making an impact on the planet, they must first have choices that would enable them to live sustainably.

On food technology

We are in a phase right now where our food system is just going through a massive transformation and alternative proteins are very much a part of that. What we're seeing globally today is that consumers are basically saying, 'Look. I want to eat healthier and that means I want to eat more plants.' Globally, about 20 per cent of consumers now call themselves flexitarians. These are people that say, 'I want to eat meat, but I want to eat more plants.' They're kind of moving away from meat but they still want to continue eating meat.

The second big thing is that the way we make food is changing. We've been engineering food for a very long time, but we engineer food using food science and ingredients. That's what these large food companies are doing when they put food in grocery stores. Now, we are making food using biotechnology and molecules, and this is completely different. It is a new game; a new type of food and new things are possible. Alternative meat choices are now created using biotechnology and molecules instead of food science and ingredients.

On Asia and alternative protein

Since I had started my life in Asia, I think some part of me really wanted to come back and live here at this point. But obviously, that is something that needed to make sense, overall, with what I was doing in my life. When I decided that I wanted to focus on alternative proteins and specifically create a VC fund focused on the sector, I decided to look at Asia because, by 2025, Asia will be the largest market in the world for alternative proteins. I specifically came to Singapore because Singapore, in that respect, is the gateway to Asia for alternative proteins. The government here has created a '30 by 30' programme that essentially focuses on creating 30 per cent of its nutrition locally by 2030. That really is an outgrowth of a lot of the food security issues that COVID highlighted.

Singapore, as a result of that, is a hotbed for innovation and for activity
in the sector. In that sense, if you want to come to Asia and enter the market,
Singapore is a very logical place to start cultivated meat, which is where you're
growing animal cells outside the animal; literally, you're growing real meat
and creating real meat outside the animal. Singapore has, for that, the most
advanced regulatory pathway in the world. It's only one of two places in the
world where it's legal to sell that in any capacity. It was the first in the world
to do so and still remains the most advanced.

On technology as catalyst for innovation

Good Startup exists to remove animals from the food system. Any time
we look at an investment, we ask ourselves, 'Is this company going to help
remove animals from our food system?', and that's our starting point. When
we speak with a company, the first question we usually ask them is, 'Tell
us about your technology. What is the technology that you have? What's
unique?' The reason that we do that is because, if you look at where we need
to go in 2050, we will not get there by doing more of what we've been doing.
We have to get there by doing something different, and to do something
different you have to innovate. Technology is that catalyst for innovation.
So that's why we start with technology. If we get comfortable with the
technology, then we start to look at the company fairly systematically.
We look at the team, at the product, at the approach to the market, at
the way that the company's been structured, at a lot of different factors.
Then we make a decision on whether we invest. Today, we have twenty-
one investments in the portfolio and again we expect that we'll get to about
thirty-five investments total in this fund.

On Good Startup's investments

Our fund looks across meat, seafood, dairy eggs as well as materials that
come from animals, principally leather but also wool and silk. In addition to
that, we invest in companies that are in the supply chain—so the companies
that are building the ingredients, the processes, and the equipment that's
needed to produce these end consumer products—so we have a fairly broad
spectrum.

One of the latest companies that we invested in is a 3D printing company
that has incredible technology that is far ahead of anything else we've seen

on the 3D printing side for food. This is a technology that would actually be scalable, and this company can print not just plant-based meat but also cultivated meat and so it can fuse those together to create a hybrid product. So imagine if you had a product where you had the nutrition of plants, you had custom proteins coming from microorganisms, and you had the taste and texture coming from animal cells. It sounds strange but, in terms of an ideal product that tastes great, it is great for the environment. That's the holy grail and I think we are getting closer and closer to that every day.

On sustainable choices

We all make choices every day that impact the planet. This happens when we turn on a light, we drive a car, we fly in an airplane, when we eat the kind of foods that we eat. We use single-use plastics. There's a lot of things we're doing that we know impact the planet. I think all of us have an inherent desire to want to do things better. To want to find a way to have a smaller impact to be able to just live more sustainably. I think a lot of us want to do that, but to do that you need choices. We need those choices. If we can create more choices, much like with automotives, you have electric cars, if we have food that tastes great but it's also more sustainable or it's healthier for you, I think that a lot of us would opt for that. I think the effort here is to really provide consumer choice to give more options to all of us so that we can eat healthier, we can eat in a way that's better for the planet. We can just live our lives in a way that we feel better about.

Fast Talk with John

I know you were born in India. Eventually, after ten years, you moved to Silicon Valley. But what makes you Asian?

I was born in India and spent the first several years of my life there. Being brought up in an Indian household through my formative years, I think certainly left an impression of the culture that's a very formative part of who I am. But at the same time, I'd like to believe that being brought up in Asia, there is a larger community there with a shared heritage. I think there is a certain outlook on the world. A certain ethos that goes well beyond the borders of countries. I very much share in that heritage. That's a big reason why I wanted to come back and live in this part of the world.

Is there anything about India that you would like for people to see or experience?

India is a place where two-thirds of the country lives in the villages. Even before independence, Mahatma Gandhi said, essentially, that if you want to get to know India, see its villages. It's hard to get to the villages sometimes because it's not a tourist attraction. Obviously, people aren't going. I was brought up in a city, not a village, but there are ways to get there—by doing things such as volunteer work. The opportunity to engage with the culture of India—and certainly the villages—are very diverse. I spent a year traveling around India and ended up doing volunteer work, specifically, so I could get to the villages. It's not a part of India that gets talked about very much but that's what I would urge people to do.

Do you have any modern-day heroes that you think deserve to be talked about?

I really admire Elon Musk a lot. You could say it's a cliché in a sense because, at the moment, he's the world's richest guy and he's pretty much out there. But the reason that I admire him is because he's had the courage to follow his own path. If you trace back his career, what you find is that he had these different experiences like us: initial startup that he did then, PayPal, and in each case, he took essentially all of his resources and he put them entirely into the next project. This is a person who is going all-in into everything he does again and again and again. That courage to follow your own path and to have a level of belief in yourself where you bet everything and you say even if it doesn't work out, I'll be fine but I'm going to give it my all, that is not something highlighted as often about him. But I really greatly admire people who have the courage to really understand who they are and try to bring that before. Because I really do think that authenticity is fundamentally an act of courage.

If you were to give a commencement speech, what message can you give to a lot of our young graduates right now who are coming into this very unpredictable world that we find ourselves in?

I consider myself an optimist. I'm a huge believer in what this next generation will do, and I think that when I talk to young folks, they really express a deep desire to make the world better; to make wonderful choices that we didn't think to make when we were at that age. That's the wonderful thing about the way that our society evolves. As far as a message that I would give in a commencement speech, I believe what the world needs most right now is compassion. We just need to have a lot more empathy and a lot more understanding about what different people are going through, what they need, what their backgrounds are, what their struggles are, because all of us have some struggles. The incredible thing about compassion is that if you truly practice compassion towards others, chances are that you will be compassionate towards yourself too. In this day and age, that turns out to be a pretty big deal too.

With COVID and with all the pressure that young folks have in this sort of new age of social media and technology and all the things that are going on with just the pace at which we live our lives, I think that self-compassion is really critical and that would go a long way towards addressing the mental health issues that are hidden underneath and go alongside the struggles that a lot of individuals have. I think there's just a lot of problems in the world that we could be better at addressing. Just when we come across people, I think there *are* opportunities to put aside the judgement and focus on understanding to listen instead of trying to shout out our point of view—and all of us are a work in progress in that respect. But I really think what we need most is compassion.

Would you like to share with us any particular thing that you do that prepares you for your day?

I start my day as much as possible with three activities. The first is journaling, the second is reading, and the third is exercise because I find those activities as a baseline to nurture my mind and body and help prepare me for the day. The way that I approach my day is that I make a ranked list of the things I need to get done and I look at those and, as much as possible, go down that list and get through as many of them as I can. The area that I would love to be better at is walking away from it and giving myself more, just simple, unstructured time off. I think it's really powerful to have time to yourself with no agenda at all. It is, in a sense, a bit scary that even when we take time off, sometimes we try to figure out everything we can stuff into it. There's an opportunity for me to at least step away and just take time. I'm trying to build that rhythm into my life too.

What is the one thing that you wish you could have known or done sooner?

I would say the power of compounding in every area of your life. It just turns out that if you decide that you're going to commit to something for a long period of time, really good things happen. It just takes time to do something great. It doesn't matter if it's learning a skill or building up your body or learning how to keep your mind quiet or building a company or nurturing a relationship. Good things just take time, and they compound. In fact, I think that if each of us were to look at our lives and we were to look at the best things about it, there's a pretty good chance that none of those things happened yesterday.

If a person really loves his or her career, if a person is in a wonderful relationship, if a person has gotten into a really good shape, that probably is the function of a fair amount of time. I would say compounding. It's simple continuity. You can almost measure your life by the degree of continuity that you have in areas that matter to you. And if you don't have that continuity, which is what I tell myself, better start; because a week later, you'll have that much continuity, and a month later you'll have more.

What would your epitaph say?

He was kind and useful. I think those are the two traits that I aspire to. More than anything else, I admire people who are kind and I would hope that I can be kind to others and to myself. When it comes to being useful, I believe that we can each be useful in different ways to different people, different causes. Whatever it is, I think that being useful improves the world. It improves people's lives. It gives us a great feeling when we can be useful, and we get to choose how we can be useful. Those are the two things that I aspire to.

If there is anything that you would like for me to try, whether it's in my entrepreneurial life or on a personal basis, anything that you do that you would like for me or anyone to try, what is that one thing that you wish you knew we could just give it a shot?

My response is a bit general here, but you may have heard this saying that 'Life is lived at the edge and it's specifically lived at the edge of our comfort zones.' There's an interesting book called *On Becoming a Person*. One of the things the author says in the book is, 'If you want to know your greatest path of personal growth, make a list of your greatest fears and go conquer them one by one.' Whatever it is that each of us can do to get to that edge and to give ourselves perspective—and it doesn't need to be something inherently out there or dangerous or something crazy. Travel gives us perspective. Reading gives us perspective. Sitting quietly gives us perspective. And trying completely new things we've never done gives us perspective. Whenever I think we have a chance to go and do something we would not have done otherwise or is something that we think will stretch us in some way, I believe there's a real argument for us to go and do that. Because, if nothing else, we'll probably end up with an interesting story but, best case, we will learn a bit more about ourselves, which I think is really precious.

My Thoughts

I loved the documentary *The Game Changers* on Netflix. Executive produced by James Cameron, Arnold Schwarzenegger, Jackie Chan, Lewis Hamilton, Novak Djokovic, and Chris Paul, the film tells the story of elite Special Forces trainer and 'The Ultimate Fighter' winner James Wilks as he travels the world on a quest to uncover the optimal diet for human performance. Maybe a lot of people were saying it was just too much, that the documentary was overstating the benefits of a plant-based diet and vilifying the animal meat industry. But *Game Changers* was effective in not just raising a lot of eyebrows, but in actually convincing people to give that lifestyle what it deserves, which is going out and modifying your diet to incorporate more plants than meat.

For now, I don't see myself ever giving up meat consumption totally, but I do make a conscious effort to widen my understanding and appreciation of other sources of protein and essential nutrients. I've taken to switching, for example, to a plant-based organic protein powder for my post-workout supplement. For the past two months, I've also been taking one to two tablespoons of Coco MCT oil, or medium chain triglycerides, along with my morning coffee or cereal to jumpstart my day.

An interesting factoid from this new routine: I've actually lost around five pounds from taking Coco MCT every morning. I had no intention of losing weight and my workouts have been pretty much the same, but I could not attribute the weight loss to anything other than my new routine. Upon further research, I came upon a non-conclusive study that apparently points to MCT oil supporting weight loss by increasing fullness, fat loss, ketone production, and improving the gut environment. Again, this is non-conclusive and should not be attributed to my consumption of MCT oil alone.

The bigger picture that I would like for myself and for others who are looking at alternatives to our always on-the-go urban diet is a greater awareness of the impact of what we eat not just to our own selves and our bodies but to the environment. People like Gautam, with his company and initiatives, have slowly been responsible for moving the needle in terms of us getting there. I applaud him for that, and I wish that there were more people like him, and more funds as well, that would dedicate their resources to trying to see how we could slow down the degradation of our planet because of what we do—and save ourselves from ourselves in the future.

Chapter Assignments

Resources on eating healthier are abundant but temptations are also everywhere. Technology is making it easier for us to have choices. You don't have to give up what you're used to eating growing up, but you can always:

- Be a flexitarian. Find healthier alternatives without fully giving up on what you have been consuming for a long time. Experiment and see what you can try that you can stick with for the long haul.
- Practice empathy. Watch documentaries that inform you of just how eating meat feeds an industry that has gone way out of hand. But always, always, take things with a grain of salt. Painting a sinister picture of entire industries is a slippery slope that one should exercise caution to objectively assess. At the end of the day, you back your beliefs with your lifestyle choices.
- Try that veggie burger! You'll never know how good it is until you try, right? Based on what I've been seeing and tasting, the alternatives are slowly but surely coming close to what we're used to.

Bibi Russell

Founder, BiBi Productions and Fashion for Development
UNESCO Artist for Peace
Ambassador of Earth Day Network Bangladesh
Bangladeshi fashion icon and former international model

'My work is to show the beauty which I see in poverty.'

'Save the craftspeople and help revive their dreams'

Armed with her goal to help revive the Bangladeshi weaving culture, former international model, Bibi Russell established in 1995 Bibi Productions Fashion for Development to save her country's craftspeople and support them in reaching for their own dreams.

Over twenty years before that, Bibi laid the roots for her organization by studying at the London College of Fashion. In 1976, during her graduation show, she not only showcased her collection but, at the insistence of her professors, modeled one of her outfits as well—and the rest, as they say, was history. Upon graduating in 1976, Bibi became one of the darlings of the modeling world in Europe; becoming the face of Vogue, Cosmopolitan, Marie Claire, and many more.

After her career as a top model that lasted until 1993, Bibi decided to go home to her native Bangladesh in 1994. Born in Tetovo to both Bangladeshi parents (her mother is from Dhaka, the country's capital, while her father is from the north), and having been given a strong Bangladeshi and Asian education, Bibi knew that it was time then to pursue what had always been her mission in life: to restore her country's weaving heritage to its former glory.

While she initially found it difficult to get Bibi Productions up and running, Bibi finally, in 1996, launched her first ready-to-wear collection aptly named Weavers of Bangladesh, at the United Nations Educational, Scientific and Cultural Organization (UNESCO) headquarters in Paris. UNESCO has been instrumental to Bibi Productions' success, supporting several of their shows in Europe, including at London Fashion Week.

To date, Bibi Productions has been able to provide work for thousands of weavers and artisans and is at the forefront of development of handloom fabrics with colours that are non-chemically produced, as Bibi is also highly conscious of the fashion industry's environmental footprint. Going beyond Bangladesh, Bibi has continued to travel the world not as a model, but as an educator of craftspeople in countries such as Africa and the Philippines, enabling them to create a more sustainable livelihood for them and their communities.

A true humanitarian by heart, Bibi likewise strives in her diligent pursuit of easing the burden of Bangladesh's street children. Her work with them has so far helped over seventy street urchins enroll in school, setting them on the path towards realizing their ambitions.

On her 'accidental' venture into modeling

Actually, modeling was not my dream. It just happened. I went to the London College of Fashion, and in the graduation show you need to show your collection with a professional model. So, my professor told me you can wear one outfit, so I wore one. And, of course, all the graduation shows are very important. People come—designers and photographers—and they are looking to find new talent because the college shows good collections. The next day, the college called me and they said, 'They want you to do modeling. Can you imagine that? There was Barbara Daly, John Frieda, Lauren Ashtyn—they want you to do modeling.' I said, 'No, no, I don't want to do it,' but the college said, 'We taught you basic grammar, and if you go around, do modeling, you can learn different techniques from different designers—but keep your mouth shut that you are a fashion designer.'

I didn't have to struggle so much in modeling because I had a particular look, and I came from a new country, Bangladesh, so people had so much curiosity about this girl. 60 per cent of the time I didn't have to go for an audition. If I had one bit of success, I owe this to Bangladesh, because it was a new country that piqued people's curiosity. Plus, I didn't have much competition, because I had a very particular look and photographers loved it. When I went to Europe, people said I'm quite tall for a Bangladeshi girl. I have eyes that are more like southeast Asians'—smaller eyes.

My first job was at Harper's Bazaar: fourteen pages with Eric Bowman who, at that time, was the best photographer. Modeling was not my dream, but it allowed me to travel all over the world and, the most important thing, led me to connect with the media who gave me support during my career. Today, they continue to give me priceless support. I'm very grateful that I learned techniques from English, French, German, New York, and Japanese designers.

Also, my travels in, say, Latin America or Central Asia, Asia has helped me know their culture. Reading about that in a book versus seeing yourself— it's completely different. So that's really helping me in what I'm doing now.

On constant learning

One day, I was in Italy, and I was saying to my friends, 'Teach me how to do graphics.' They were saying, 'Are you mad? You are doing modeling; why do you want to learn?'

I'm still learning. I think the learning process never stops. Doesn't matter how old you are, or how experienced you are. I was born and brought up until a certain age in Bangladesh—early teenage years—then I went to Europe. So, I know that Asian culture, our culture. I remain grounded because at home, my parents taught me about Asian culture. So, when I went to Europe, I never forgot my roots and that is important. My parents never taught me that you are going to be the star in the sky. I looked at the stars and I learned many things about them through books and poetry, and songs and many, many, many artists. And I'm so lucky to have learned many things from my home. My parents didn't force me to return to Bangladesh, but they knew I would go back with certain things because I learned many things from Europe through traveling.

I learned how to make handmade paper in the Philippines. I've been many times in your country—it is so beautiful. So, in every country, there is something we can learn.

On fulfilling her dream

Everyone has a dream. I grew up in Bangladesh with so many sights to see; people in beautiful *saris* or *sarong*, wearing nice bangles. So, I used to look at my many coloured pencils and think, they can look much better in different colour combinations. These gave me a dream, which grew with me. I am a Bangladeshi girl who comes from a family where everyone is a doctor or engineer—and I studied fashion. I knew my dream was clear why I came to Europe and why I studied.

I came back from Italy to Bangladesh in 1994, and back then I thought, this is a mistake. I thought that when I did Bibi Productions, I would immediately get the support I was getting all over the world. But being Asian, when you come home from Europe with a bit of success, people think you will buy a home, big cars, and that you have lots of money. So, I started working from zero again, so people used to think she's crazy. She doesn't live in a big house, no big car. People thought, 'Bibi Russell, you're so famous. Why do you want to do that?' So you see that? So, I opened Bibi Productions with the hope that maybe I will get support, but it's 100 per cent funded by my own money; whatever I earn in my life, I put in it. But seeing how many people I am able to work with, that gives me the strength to continue. My mental satisfaction is here; when I go to your country or Latin America, they never made me feel that I have no money. My biggest strength is my work that is absolutely linked with development, sustainability, and craftspeople throughout the world. They know that I respect their human dignity.

On educating and honouring the dignity of those living in marginalized societies

My work is to show the beauty which I see in poverty. When I go in the villages, even in the Philippines, you see the people, and maybe they are not rich, but they have a smile to die for. They have two eyes like stars. I love craftspeople all over the world. I have worked in so many countries; when I go to your country, the first thing I say is, 'Don't make me a foreigner. I'm part of you.'

I respect their dignity; that's number one. I never say 'poor', I say 'village people', so they know I respect them. You can be poor, but you can come out of poverty. Look at me. I'm from Bangladesh.

Another thing. Suppose I'm going to the Philippines. You invite me to go and work with your craftspeople. First thing I will say is, 'Can I go around, see what resources you have?' I will work with you; I will never buy things from China or Japan or India or Bangladesh. I make sure you use your local ingredients.

Also, I am an artist. I love your shirt, but I'm not stupid enough to copy exactly that. By simply copying, you cannot help a country come out of poverty. I make them realize, the village people, that I'm not a donor agency. I'm not going there and giving you money. I make them realize that if you don't have the education, you give your children that education. Instead of having five children, have two, three children. I don't force them; I make them realize—that's very, very important. And during this pandemic, I make sure that they don't throw away chemicals here and there. Environmental pollution—I go to the villages for months to make them understand this.

I want to share one story in Africa. The first person who believed in me was, for twelve years, UNESCO Director General Federico Mayor. So, I was asked to work in Africa, and Mr Mayor said, 'You give your support to UNESCO,'—and they supported me.

I understand French, but I don't understand the African way of speaking French. He sent me to Mali where they make beautiful, beautiful rags. I went with the UNESCO research team and discovered this elderly guy who makes beautiful rags. I went with an interpreter from UNESCO, and I asked how much it is. For the four by six rags, he said $2,000, so I told him, 'Please tell me how long it took you to make that.' 'Why are you asking?' he said. 'That is the price!' He got very angry with me because they can sell that within two days—and then for six months they can eat with that money. He said, 'I don't want to talk with you, you come for me, and you want to know my secret?' He shut that door.

So, I went back. I'm also not giving up. The next day we went, I tried to be friendly and everything, make him understand. It took me more than ten days to make him see that I am giving you sustainable development, that you don't wait for two days for someone to buy. I will make sure that you make money. That was my biggest achievement: I worked there on and off for one year, and he said, 'I'm sorry I gave you such a hard time—you are the mother

of craftspeople from all over the world.' That person who didn't want to
share anything, after ten days, the way he hugged me—I can still remember
that even if it was more than twelve years ago. That you can get that kind of
love and affection is priceless.

On the important impact of slow fashion

I'm trying till the end to make the world understand: there is machine-made,
there is handmade. When you eat at home something cooked by your mother
or your wife or your sister, it's something else; but sometimes you eat fast
food too. That's the kind of satisfaction that I want to give them through my
work. Mine is completely slow fashion.

If you support craftspeople you will see—go around your villages. It's not
one person you are giving to, but a family who can come out of poverty. With
my work, I want to show the people all over the world that craftspeople have
magical fingers; to get that magical work, you have to respect their dignity.
They will do fantastic. We are a very small organization and self-funded; no
one funds us because I don't write proposals, I don't have time. But people
are coming out of poverty with dignity. They're working heads up. They're
smiling. This is what I always say. I want to save the craftspeople and help
revive their dreams.

On helping children achieve a better life for themselves

I am helping most of the children who are living below the poverty line,
because I've talked to them, as I spend a lot of time with them all over in
Bangladesh. I listen to them to talk about what their dreams are. Another
thing, John—I was not a beautiful Bangladeshi. I'm tall and skinny and dark,
so I used to listen to the whole world that used to tell me, 'She's so ugly.'
But it didn't affect me. And now, when I go around villages, I see there are
girls who are like me, and they have other younger sisters, and the parents
complain to me about how they will find someone to marry them, they're
going to ask for a lot of dowry money. So, I tell them, your daughter can be
doing something better. They can do so many things. Education, I tell them,
you have to give them basic education. There are many NGOs that offer free
schooling. I signed up as their guardian.

Fast Talk with John

What makes you Bangladeshi?

What makes me Bangladeshi? My smile. That is what the world doesn't know. Even in the poorest area, they smile and you can see those little eyes twinkling.

Is there anything from your country that you would like the world to know about or discover?

First of all, I would like to invite you to come by and then you will understand my people. Bangladesh, yes, there have been so many political disasters, but there is a good side. The beauty of Bangladesh, you have to come and see. Every part of it, you have to cross a river or a body of water. The people—you have to come and see what I mean, that the people will show you their absolute strength.

Who, to you, is a superhero?

Rabindranath Tagore, the Bengali poet, short-story writer, song composer, playwright, essayist, and painter who became the first non-European to receive the Nobel Prize for Literature in 1913. He wrote our national anthem. He's my superhero of all time.

If you could give a commencement speech (if you haven't already), what message would you want to impart?

I would say to the young generation, as I see that the world is going digital, that personal touch is different. Also, you are much faster than me in getting information about the world—please start with your own cultural heritage.

Go for your dream. Be focused.

How do you prepare for what you do? Any special routines you can share?

I am vegetarian, and I have a very simple life. I try to do a little bit of meditation, my own meditation. And I never take any medicine. When I get up in the morning, I sit and I just block myself. I just think, today's the day to do what I want to do.

What would your epitaph say?

That I was at the heart of craftspeople. If I am born again, I want to be doing exactly what I have done. I think that that is the only thing because one lifetime is not enough.

If there is anything specific you do that you would recommend I try, what would it be?

Look around at the talented young generation, and give them support, motivate them. They are the future.

My Thoughts

What Bibi does with her social enterprise, framed against the context of a globalized economy where it's so easy to get something that's commercial and readily available, is amazing and truly admirable. It's completely slow; the opposite direction that fast fashion has dictated most of the world to go. In fact, her creations are heirloom pieces that can be passed on from generation to generation. And each piece of clothing puts food on the table of the craftsperson's family that night.

I really appreciate what Bibi has shared and most especially her outlook on uplifting people. I think it is a very noble cause and one that has to be considered, outside the realms of fashion. I believe that, in this day and age, where there's so much focus on making more, producing more, doing more. I think it's just beautiful how what Bibi does impacts so many people, and allows them to have dignity, while having a sustainable business.

If I were to equate this to my own enterprise, how do I make sure that I am also able to provide opportunities for the marginalized to participate in nation building? I've seen my peers from other industries, for example, hire senior citizens or single mothers, and persons with disabilities. What is it that we do in our own organization that can allow for us to extend the impact of what we do to include those that have been ostracized or are not given the same opportunities? This is something that we, as an organization, must be mindful of and actually take on as an advocacy.

Chapter Assignments

Bibi Productions is all about helping people create a more sustainable way of life for themselves. Create a plan for how you can contribute to environmental sustainability by trying these simple things:

- Go slow. Patronize brands that promote slow fashion, and purchase pieces that are timeless and durable so as to avoid frequent shopping.
- Choose your plastic. Plastic is not all bad, especially since it is a convenient tool for packaging and storage. Choose plastic that is also more long-lasting and recyclable so as to minimize your carbon footprint.
- If you have a business or work for a company with a manufacturing component, try to see how you can integrate the nearby communities into your value chain. It can be as simple as sourcing raw materials they can provide or hiring a certain subset of marginalized communities such as senior citizens or persons with disabilities.

Nameeta Dargani

Founding Member and President, Art of Living Foundation, Philippines

'Find the opportunity within yourself to bring out the valour in you.'

Creating a ripple effect of individual peace

Nameeta Dargani is the founding member and President of the Art of Living Foundation, which is an international non-profit educational and humanitarian organization with presence in about 156 countries. It is the largest volunteer-run organization in the world that leads various humanitarian efforts and service initiatives, including peace building, conflict resolution, prisoner rehabilitation, and environmental sustainability. The organization also offers programmes that equip people with the tools and techniques that they need to manage their mind and emotions and to facilitate the elimination of stress—through very powerful breathing techniques and meditation yoga, plus some practical wisdom to navigate life's daily challenges. Art of Living was founded by Sri Sri Ravi Shankar, a world-renowned peace ambassador, humanitarian, and a spiritual teacher.

Dargani has a business degree from the European Business School London. Dargani hails from Mumbai but moved to the Philippines when she was thirteen. At present, she teaches the Art of Living Happiness Programme in the Philippines wherein she guides people who manage stress using breathing techniques, meditation, and yoga.

On her training under Sri Sri Ravi Shankar

I feel so fortunate because even as a teenager I wanted to help, I wanted to do something to have my life be more meaningful. But I didn't know how, and I didn't have any structure as to how to contribute. When I did the Art of Living programme back in 2005, I was introduced to Sri Sri Ravi Shankar, and I was so moved because I could see someone working tirelessly with a very simple vision of just wanting to see a smile on every face. He travels to over forty countries a year. Traveling the world and showing that just by attaining that individual sense of peace within us, we can then share it and that can create a ripple effect and influence all of society. He walks the talk, and he is constantly working for this cause. He's very involved in conflict resolution, works with governments and various organizations. He just exudes such a sense of peace and calm and wisdom.

At the same time, there's a lightness about him; usually when someone is very wise and full of knowledge, you tend to feel a little bit overwhelmed but with him you know you can just be yourself. He has a lot of humour and wit, and I just feel so fortunate.

Sri Sri is such an amazing example of service being available to the need of the moment.

On stress, breathing, and meditation

What brought me to the programme was I was suffering from terrible back pain back in 2005. It was really interfering with the quality of my life. There were so many things I couldn't do. Simple things like getting in and out of the car. I had to negotiate every move. It was quite frustrating, and I was stuck in a cycle of stress. Negative emotions that were coming as a result of stress and then just being miserable. On one hand, life was great. I was happily married with two sons, and I had everything I wanted. But something was missing and a lot of it was also induced by the physical pain.

When I learned the techniques, Sky Meditation in particular, the Sudarshan Kriya Yoga technique, I was able to finally break out of that cycle of stress and the muscle spasms. What would happen is when I would get stressed, my muscles would go into spasm and that was obviously very painful and that sets off an emotional reaction.

In learning how to breathe I was able to finally de-link from all of that and just come back into a space of calm. My muscles would just naturally relax and I'd feel so much better in a few days. I found that I relaxed as I became more calm, and things started to shift even on a mental level and emotional level. My mind just got so much clearer. I was more focused. I was getting things done a lot faster. Smiling a lot. Just being happy.

This was so wonderful. I thought everyone needs to learn this. As simple as breathing. We have this tendency to think that when our problems are so complex, they also require complex solutions but actually we have with us a tool that is within reach; free, user-friendly, and available to you all the time. If we could only tap into this, it could totally transform our lives.

On sources of energy

Exercise is a huge source of energy. There are many sources of energy and if we could tap into those, then we could increase our energy levels naturally rather than reaching out for that triple shot of espresso. We could naturally increase our energy levels.

There are four main sources of energy. The first one is food, the most obvious source of energy but the right type of food (fresh vegetables and fruits) and in the right quantity. And then sleep is a big one. So, the right amount of sleep is also important. If you sleep too much you tend to feel sluggish as well and if you sleep too little, we all know how that feels. The third source of energy is our breath. It is the one that is just not looked into as much as it should be. We're just not optimizing this source of energy in our lives. If you think about it, we're breathing all the time and the breath is a way for us to bring in more life force energy into our system. If we optimize our breath, if we expand our lung capacity, we can actually be so much more efficient not only at increasing our energy but also in detoxifying our system.

On how breathing lets you be in the moment

Have you noticed that the mind tends to vacillate between the past and the future? When the mind is in the past, very often emotions come up like guilt, anger. Anger is always about something that happened in the past, or regret. When the mind goes to the future, it's about anxiety, worry, and fear. This constant vacillation of the mind creates a lot of stress in the nervous system—but where is joy, where is happiness? Where is enthusiasm and creativity? All of that is happening here in the present moment.

We know there's nothing new about this; there are books written about the power of now and so on, but how do we bring our mind to the present moment when our experience tells us that it's so difficult to do? When you go through the breath, it becomes easier because your breath is more tangible than the mind; you can actually work with your breath. You can think of the breath as your mind, which is like a kite flying all over the place, going to the past, going to the future. Your breath is like that string that helps you to bring the mind back again and again to the present moment and anchors you there. There are breathing techniques that we teach, and you'll find that it's easier to stay present and stay anchored in the moment, and there's less tendency to constantly vacillate between the past and the future, which doesn't really serve us and yet so much time of the day we spend in regret in anger and guilt and we get stuck—that's the problem.

Breathing helps us return to the present moment, and it's also the connecting link between the mind and the body. If you'll notice, when you experience different emotions, they each have a corresponding breath pattern. When you're angry you breathe in a different way compared to when you're calm and relaxed—this is actually the premise of the Sudarshan Kriya technique that we teach. It's actually a two-way street when we work with our breath; when we use our breath, when we manipulate the breath, when we breathe in different patterns, we can then influence our state of mind and our emotions, and this is why it's so effective.

On the Seven Levels of Existence—and how to centre one's Self

1. Body: The most obvious level of our existence; the physical level.
2. Breath
3. Mind: The faculty through which we perceive the world around us through the five senses.
4. Intellect: Where we judge, analyse.
5. Memory
6. Ego and emotions
7. Self

The Self is that ultimate level of our existence. It's such an important part of us, yet many of us don't spend time in that level of our existence. When we meditate, we do these breathing techniques that take us to that level of the self—the seventh level of our existence. When we spend time on that level, we harmonize all the other levels of our existence, and then somehow during your day, yes, things will happen, stressors will come, life will throw a curveball at you—but at least you're equipped. You know you've done your practice; you've centred yourself. When we feel like we're overwhelmed and we're drowning, why not be proactive about it and start a practice where you regularly do some breathing, some meditation? This prepares you, so that whatever happens, it's not so easy to take away your smile.

Fast Talk with John

What makes you Asian?

Here in Asia, we have these wonderful values of respect for family and just being there with the family unit. I love that about being Asian. There's also a wonderful sense of hospitality that you find when you travel around Asia. This warm and welcoming sense that you get anywhere you go. There is also this spiritual aspect whenever you travel around Asia. You feel it. It may be different in terms and different religions but there's some wisdom, some spirituality that you find. Food, of course, I love Asian food.

Is there anything from the Philippines that you would like for the world to discover or about India for that matter?

For the Philippines, we have the best beaches in the world for sure. There's no doubt about that. I really think we have some stunning beaches. I love traveling around the Philippines. Filipinos are naturally so warm and friendly and managed to just keep this happy attitude no matter what's going on.

For India, I was born in Mumbai and I spent my formative years there. I have a very deep connection to India. For me, the most important thing is the depth of spirituality. A lot of people travel to India to gain these insights, to learn the wisdom of the ancient masters. I feel very fortunate that I grew up in that tradition. India has a lot to offer in terms of that depth of spirituality and knowledge and wisdom. And of course, Indian food is the best.

Is anyone out there who to you is a modern-day hero? Who would that person be and what qualities he or she possess that would make that person in your eyes a modern hero?

For me, that's really easy. I told you in the beginning I was completely taken by the amazing book and dedication of the founder of Art of Living Sri Sri Ravi Shankar who, to me, embodies love. The love that I'm talking about is this sense of love wherever he goes you just feel that he exudes that and just watching him, learning from him, having had the chance to be in his presence and be around him has been such an influence in my own life.

If you would ever give a commencement speech in school right now, what message would you have for graduates particularly now in these difficult times?

I would say that even in difficult times, even in adversity, there's always a good side. Have you noticed when there's a natural disaster how communities just band together? People who may not normally go out of their way, but you find them in evacuation centres and they're packing relief goods. This brings out qualities of sharing and generosity and resilience. We are in a state of adversity with this pandemic going on but with a state like that, there's always a good side; there's always an opportunity and find the opportunity within yourself to bring out the qualities, bring out the valour in you.

My Thoughts

I've always been fascinated with the science of the breath and its benefits, and though I've had some experience at different points in time—whether in school, on retreats, even on professional executive programmes and conferences—the Art of Living Happiness Programme's Sudarhan Kriya was time well spent just focused on the activity of mindfulness and breathing for its own sake.

Before we started the programme, Nameeta asked me three things:

1. What do you want in life?
2. What are the things that bother you?
3. What do you expect to gain from this course?

Note that I took this programme—a few hours a day spread out over four sessions—neck deep in the pandemic, when all of Manila was locked down. These were days when I was hardly sleeping, with thoughts of the future and how to handle the business and with an abruptly disrupted house construction clouding my psyche at the time.

One has to engage in a class to truly understand and gain first-hand exposure of the breathing techniques of the Sudarshan Kriya method.

The Ujayi Breathing technique, also called the ocean sounding breath (I prefer thinking of it as the Darth Vader breathing technique), for one, is a great way to calm your mind by focusing on your breath.

On my *Methods to Greatness* podcast, I got on an actual session with Nameeta as we went through this along with other breathing exercises such as the Bhastrika Pranayama, deep abdominal breathing or Yogi breath, and the Bee Breath, which is my personal favourite. There are so much more that can best be experienced through video as it involves sounds and specific timings. I highly recommend you check out the Nameeta Dargani episode. *Methods to Greatness* by John Aguilar podcast is available on Spotify, Apple Podcast, and on all platforms where you get your regular podcast fix.

Chapter Assignments

The noise of our lives exacerbated by social media and other distractions in our hyperconnected world makes it difficult for us to tune in to ourselves. Our souls need to tune out from all these so we can exercise mental hygiene and rejuvenate. Here are a few things you may want to consider doing to help you find balance from within:

- Sudarshan Kriya, Transcendental Meditation (TM), yoga, whatever form you choose, can help immensely in your search for clarity and a way to be able to combat stress. Read up, take classes, and try to discover what's best for you.
- A simple technique would be to breath in through your nose for four counts, hold for another four, and breath out also through your nose for six counts, hold for two and start again. Do this for eight sets.
- Nameeta's advice to us: perform three random acts of kindness a day. You'll never know, a small random act of kindness can be the life changing words or break that can totally change someone else's life. 'What have you done to bring out divine qualities in others?'

My Soul Journey

I recently went on a week-long trip to Israel upon the invitation of the Ambassador of Israel to the Philippines, Ilan Fluss. My eight-day sojourn was a flurry of activities, meetings and events in Tel Aviv that were designed for me to have an appreciation of Israeli technologies, and to see how I could help bridge innovation between our two countries. In between those meetings, I was able to go on a weekend trip to Jerusalem.

Jerusalem is on the bucket list of a lot of Catholic Filipinos and though I am Catholic, I must say that apart from what I would read about in the Bible when in elementary school, Jerusalem was not a place that was on my bucket list of places to go to or see before I die. It was nonetheless a rich experience that was good for my soul as it gave me the chance to witness how the Jewish people were reciting their prayers in the Old City's Wailing Wall or Western Wall, shop in the Mahene Yehuda Market, and swim in the nearby Dead Sea.

But what was a spiritual encounter for me happened not in Jerusalem but back in Tel Aviv. An Israeli who I met in Manila years back by the name of Benny Shlick, founder of Innovation Without Borders, a consulting agency that bridges the Israeli innovation and tech ecosystem to the rest of the world, wanted to introduce me to his friend Adi Rosenfeld. He sent me a Forbes article on Adi that came out a couple of years back. Adi was called 'The Israeli Whisperer', was an astute reader of people's souls, and a mentor to the people he chose. There was no specific agenda for the meeting, but Benny reassured me that I should meet Adi.

Benny asked me to meet him at a co-working facility about 20 minutes from my hotel, and when I got there introduced me to a man who looked like a wise prophet from the Bible. Benny then introduces us. 'John, meet Adi. Adi, this is John.' After shaking hands, Adi led me to a nearby conference room, and we each took a chair across from each other. He looked into my eyes, and after a few moments, asked, 'Why are you here?'

For a minute, I did not know what he meant and I proceeded to tell him that I was invited by the Israel Ambassador on this innovation exchange trip to bridge our two countries. I could sense it was not the answer he was looking for. Without taking his gaze away from my eyes, he asked again, 'Why are you here?'

I took a pause for what seemed like an eternity, and after a few moments I eventually said, 'I don't know what to do.' After a few more moments, I could feel my eyes slowly welling with tears.

Adi continues, 'We've only known each other a few minutes but there is something about you. I can sense you are a very charismatic person, but you are also very lonely.'

I then proceeded to share that I was, indeed, lonely, and that a problem with my wife that surfaced just that morning made him catch me at a bad time. I was flying back to Manila that evening, and I was not in a good place. 'The problem with your wife, that is just the tip of the iceberg. There is something deeper.' He shares that he had a very difficult childhood, was abused by his parents, and caused him to stutter for most of his life. 'But you are stronger than me,' he says. 'If you have a problem, you continue to function. If I have a problem I cannot function.'

He then said something I was totally unprepared for. 'In a month, or a month and a half, I will invite you to come back to Israel, and I will invite you to be my friend. You can stay in my house for three days; you will stay in my guest house and be my guest. You don't have to worry. I will take care of everything. And during your stay I will invite people. These are very important people. You will meet them, and you will decide after that, we will organize a delegation and bring them to the Philippines.'

He continues, 'I do not know what it is about you, but you are destined for great things. But you have to open yourself up first. Only when you are open can you allow these things to come in.' I nodded in silence as I was struggling to hold back my tears.

He asks his final question. 'What do you want?'

'I just want to be happy,' I finally say.

'Whatever it is you are doing, you can stop your train. The world will wait. Do it for yourself.' he said as we concluded our brief meeting.

I left that co-working space not knowing what hit me. It was as if I had just had one of the most important albeit short meetings of my life. Not so much because of the business prospects of what Adi had promised, but more so the possibility of enriching my soul as a result.

As I write this, I have not yet booked my plane tickets back to Tel Aviv. I am certain though, at the right time when I am ready, I will stop my train, and I shall return.

I find that this section of the book, this section of the soul, is the shortest; perhaps because it is the part that I am still grappling with and trying to learn more about. I know that my younger years were mostly spent enhancing my mind and my body. At some point, as I enter the next season of my life, I know the scales will tip to wanting to enhance and connect with my soul. As I personally go up Maslow's hierarchy of needs, self-actualization—the desire to become the most that one can be—is the final frontier. And with it comes the lack of prejudice, of acceptance, of love. This is where I would like to be. I believe I still have a long way to go, but I am looking forward to the journey as much as the destination.

Act 3: Soul Key Takeaways

This section has truly been food for the soul and has allowed me to examine realms beyond the practical preoccupations and responsibilities of my day to day. I take with me these key takeaways that I hope inspires you as much as they have inspired me:

'You have to be serious about it and you have to put your skills in, you have to put all the goodness, all the positive energy and everything you want to put into your music. But that's it, don't get it bigger than your head. Don't believe in your own promotion.'

—Anggun

'But for our youth, it's a radical, liberating feeling to dare to speak amid the storm and waves, to find a constant notion, an idea that is so badly needed in the world that centuries later people might return to because you've reshaped the way we envision solving a particular problem or circumstance. Not everything you write will meet these criteria, but it's infinitely rewarding when you find the words that do.'

—Bryan Thao Worra

'There's a lot of things we're doing that we know impact the planet . . . To want to find a way to have a smaller impact to be able to just live more sustainably. I think a lot of us want to do that, but to do that you need choices . . . I think the effort here is to really provide consumer choice to give more options to all of us so that we can eat healthier, we can eat in a way that's better for the planet.'

—Gautam Godhwani

'If you support craftspeople you will see—go around your villages. It's not one person you are giving to, but a family who can come out of poverty. With my work, I want to show the people all over the world that craftspeople have magical fingers; to get that magical work, you have to respect their dignity. They're working heads up. They're smiling. This is what I always say. I want to save the craftspeople and help revive their dreams.'

—Bibi Russell

'The Self is that ultimate level of our existence. It's such an important part of us, yet many of us don't spend time in that level of our existence. When we meditate, we do these breathing techniques that take us to that level of the self—the seventh level of our existence. When we spend time on that level, then we harmonize all the other levels of our existence, and then somehow during your day, yes, things will happen, stressors will come, life will throw a curveball at you—but at least you're equipped . . . This prepares you, so that whatever happens, it's not so easy to take away your smile.'

— Nameeta Dargani

Acknowledgements

At the end of the day, when all is said and done, I would like for my epitaph to say that I have been a good son, brother, husband, and father—everything in the sequence I have been to the most important people in my life. To my father Dave and late mother Ellie, thank you for bringing me to the world and for raising me the best way you could. To my siblings Len and Martin, thank you for being there for good and bad, I will always be here for you. To my wife Monica, thank you for being my constant and for all your patience, love, and understanding. To my children Danielle, Luis and David, thank you for your love and acceptance.

I would also like to thank my second family, my team at Streetpark Productions and Dragon's Nest. Our ever-reliable mother hen Leng Bulabos for always managing to keep things together. Our head of production Don Pira, Editors Eugene, Khai Faune and Jun for journeying with me for each and every podcast episode of *Methods to Greatness*.

To my writing and research team Annelle, Rizza, and Marlet, thank you for helping me put everything together for this book.

Special thanks to our Podcast Network Asia family led by the inimitable Ronster Baetiong and his team. Francis Concio for composing the *Methods to Greatness* score.

I would also like to thank all of my guests and interviewees on *Methods to Greatness* for sharing your lives and methods to greatness with me and all our listeners, viewers, and readers. In particular those who I chose to include in this book:

Anggun
Inbal Arieli
Minh Bui
Jessica Chen
Toby Claudio
Namita Dargani
Rovilson Fernandez
Chien Han How
Gautam Godhwani
Jose Magsaysay Jr.
Dov Moran
Ernest John 'EJ' Obiena
Chot Reyes
Bibi Russell
James Soh
Dennis Anthony Uy
Brandon Vera
Bryan Thao Worra
Pia Wurtzbach
Kenichi 'Kent' Yoshida

To my publisher Penguin Random House, Nora Abu Bakar and her team, thank you for the trust and for the opportunity to share the greatness of these people I interviewed in this book to the world.